Change-Agent Skills A:
Assessing and Designing Excellence

Change-Agent Skills A:
Assessing and Designing Excellence

Gerard Egan, Ph.D.

University Associates, Inc.
8517 Production Avenue
San Diego, California 92121

Library of Congress Cataloging-in-Publication Data

Egan, Gerard.
    Change-agent skills A.

    Companion to: Change-agent skills B: managing innovation and change.
    Bibliography: p.
    Includes index.
    1. Organizational effectiveness. 2. Excellence.
I. Egan, Gerard. Change-agent skills B. II. Title.
HD58.9.E37 1988   658.4   88-10653
ISBN 0-88390-219-2

Managing Editor: Mary Kitzmiller
Jacket Designer: Janet F. Colby
Production Artists: Janet F. Colby and William Bellomy

Preface

I often ask the people who manage the corporations, businesses, institutions, and agencies for which I provide consultancy services, the following question. "Would it be useful to have a relatively simple and straightforward shared model, framework, or template that can be used by everyone within your enterprise to assess how things are going, to facilitate their work, and to design new projects?" They inevitably answer yes. However, when I put them to work to come up with the framework that they think is already in place or with one that would be useful were it in place, the product they come up with, even in their own judgment, leaves much to be desired. This should not be considered odd. Society has a way of leaving important things to chance. When I ask people in general how important—on a scale from zero to one hundred—such things as human-relations and problem-solving skills are for their children, they inevitably suggest ratings near one hundred. However, when I ask them to name the forums in which these skills are explicitly taught, they mumble something that sounds like, "These are the kinds of things that are 'picked up' along the way," knowing full well that very many do not pick them up along the way. Both in society in general and in the business and social institutions that make it work, we leave certain key skills to chance. How many managers are promoted to their posts because of their professional and technical abilities, not because they are good at managing both business and organizational processes and the people of the enterprise?

The assumption of this book is that it is quite useful, if not essential, to have a simple, yet comprehensive, shared framework for understanding business, organizational, management, and leadership realities. The framework acts as a map or guide for understanding the often complex realities of any enterprise, whether for profit or not for profit. It is not that many enterprises do not have some kind of implicit model or template. They do, but I think that there are many advantages to having an explicit framework.

The design-facilitation-assessment framework outlined in these pages has been invaluable for me in the consulting work I do. It has also proved useful for the many managers who have passed through my courses at Loyola University. This model and the change model elaborated in the companion to this book (*Change-Agent Skills B: Managing Innovation and Change*) can act as "primers" for change agents of every ilk, managers, consultants, and trainers, as they go about the task of formulating their own.

Gerard Egan

Loyola University of Chicago
March 1, 1988

Contents

1
Introduction and Overview

Many books and articles that describe excellence in companies and institutions do not offer suggestions to executives, managers, and supervisors on ways to incorporate excellence into the system. That is, they deal with the principles rather than the pragmatics of excellence. This book offers a model, called simply "Model A," for assessing excellence and for designing excellence into the system. Its companion, *Change-Agent Skills B: Managing Innovation and Change* (Egan, 1988), presents a model for the management of corporate and institutional change, called "Model B."

Although there are many models for dealing with organizational change, there are comparatively few that deal with system design and assessment (for examples, see Pascale & Athos, 1981; Kotter, 1978; Nadler & Tushman, 1977; and Weisbord, 1976). Some design and assessment frameworks are too complex, whereas others are not comprehensive enough. Some focus almost exclusively on organizational structure and say little about business dimensions such as mission, strategy, operations, and management. Model A is comprehensive without being overly complex. It presents strategic, operational, organizational, managerial, and leadership dimensions in a logical, all-purpose framework that can be used to design or assess the following:

- An entire company or institution.
- Any division of the company or institution.
- Any department of a division.
- Any unit within a department.
- Any project or program within any of the above-mentioned categories.

1

Each of these categories is a system in its own right, even though it is a part of a larger system. When Model A is used to design or assess any kind of subunit or project, it addresses the issue of linkage of the unit or project to other subunits and to the overall company or institution. Model A is dynamic in the sense that it portrays the people in an organization as transforming inputs into outputs (see Figure 1-1). Outputs, whether products or services, that satisfy the needs of clients or customers in viable markets constitute the heart of the model.

THE DISTINCTION BETWEEN AN ORGANIZATION AND A BUSINESS

The distinction between a business and an organization can be extremely useful. A company or institution is successful when it establishes a niche in the marketplace and satisfies the relevant and legitimate needs and wants of its customers or clients (regardless of what they are called: patients, parishioners, students, etc.) within its markets efficiently with products or services (this is called *productivity*) and does so while meeting the legitimate needs and wants of the people who work within the system (this is called *quality of work life*). The business dimensions of a company focus on markets, customers, mission, the products or services that satisfy customers' needs and wants, and the systems in the environment (for instance, competitors) that affect the delivery of products or services. The business focus is *outward*.

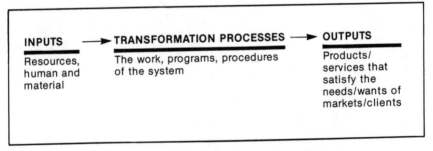

Figure 1-1. Transforming Inputs into Outputs

The organizational focus, on the other hand, is *inward*. It is the way the company or institution structures itself, its human resources, and its organizational processes in order to engage in its business. The organization exists to foster both productivity and quality of work life. This distinction is useful, not just in business and industry, but in not-for-profit, human-service, educational, and church institutions and agencies. The quality of products and services of a company or institution—whether the manufacture and sale of automobiles, the teaching and learning of mathematics, the maintenance of highways, or the presentation of liturgy—is, in a broad sense, a *business* concern. This is business in the sense that is meant when people—in *any* kind of corporation, company, institution, or agency—say, "Let's get down to business!"

Some companies and institutions become too preoccupied with inner concerns. The organization becomes an end in itself to the detriment of the business, that is, to the detriment of the development of markets and the satisfaction of the needs and wants of customers and clients in these markets through products and services. Thus there is a need for a book such as this one, which addresses itself to "getting the business into the organization." In designing and changing companies and institutions, executives, managers, and consultants must assure that the business gets into the guts of the organization so that the organization can effectively serve the business or mission of the system. The following questions will help in distinguishing between the business and the organizational structures that are meant to support the business:

- In what ways do we have a clear idea of what "business" we are in and what our business outcomes are in terms of delivering products and/or services?

- To what extent is it clear to us that our organization—in its structure, processes, and procedures—exists only to support our business?

- In what ways do organizational issues distract us and detract from the delivery of business outcomes?

- How effective are we in linking changes in organizational structure, processes, and procedures to improvement in the delivery of business outcomes?

AN OVERVIEW OF MODEL A

Model A has four major parts: business dimensions, organizational dimensions, leadership, and managing the shadow side of the organization. Each part contains a number of elements.

I. Business Dimensions

The business dimensions of Model A focus on the establishment of markets and the delivery of quality products or services to clients or customers. There are both strategic and operational business dimensions.

Strategic Business Elements

The strategic business elements give direction and purpose to the company or institution. They include the following:

• **Markets, Customers, Clients.** Viable markets need to be identified; customer needs and wants within these markets need to be explored.

• **Business Environment.** The business environment—competition, economic and social trends, new markets, emerging technology—needs to be scanned frequently for threats and opportunities.

• **Mission.** A business mission or overall purpose needs to be developed together with a parallel and integrated *people* mission.

• **Business Philosophy.** An integrated set of values and policies needs to be formulated to govern the conduct of business.

• **Major Business Categories.** The major categories of products or services to be delivered to customers in selected markets need to be determined.

• **Basic Financing.** The system needs to be established on a solid financial foundation. Many enterprises, poorly capitalized, fail before they really get off the ground.

• **Strategic Plan.** All these elements need to be addressed and pulled together into a strategic plan that sets the longer-term direction and goals of the system.

Chapters 2 through 6 deal with the strategic business dimensions.

Operational Business Elements

Operational business elements refer to the day-to-day business of the company or institution. They include the following:

• **Products/Services.** Specific high-quality products and/or services that meet the needs and wants of customers need to be designed, manufactured, marketed, and delivered.

• **Work Programs.** Step-by-step work programs that assure the efficient production and delivery of high-quality products and/or services need to be developed.

• **Material Resources.** Effective programs for choosing and using the material resources, including financial resources, to be used in work programs need to be established.

• **Unit Performance Plan.** Each unit has its own set of operations that contribute directly or indirectly to the delivery of products and services to customers. The unit performance plan sets year-long operational priorities for the unit and links operations to the overall strategy of the enterprise.

Chapters 7 through 10 deal with the operational business dimensions.

II. Organizational Dimensions

The organizational dimensions include the structure of the organization, that is, functional units and subunits, and the deployment and utilization of human resources within these units. They include the following:

- **Structure and the Division of Labor.** Functional work units need to be established. Within these units, roles with clear-cut job descriptions and responsibilities need to be set up.

- **Competence.** The units and the people working in the units must be competent, that is, capable of achieving business outcomes. Once jobs with clear-cut job descriptions are established, competent and compatible people need to be hired into these jobs and effectively socialized into the culture of the organization.

- **Teamwork.** Processes need to be established to ensure that units and people within units work together in teams whenever working together will deliver better business outcomes.

- **Communication.** Since communication is the lifeblood of the system, the organizational culture must call for (and individuals must have the skills needed for) effective information sharing, feedback, appraisal, problem solving, innovation, and conflict management among both units and individuals in units.

- **Reward System.** Incentives to do all the above must be provided, disincentives must be controlled, and performance rather than nonperformance must be rewarded.

- **Individual Performance Plans.** A sense of strategy or direction must permeate the entire system. Individual performance plans, established through dialog between individuals and their supervisors, focus yearly work priorities for each person in the system. These plans link individual efforts to the unit performance plan and—through this plan—to the overall strategy of the system.

III. Management and Leadership

If all the above is to happen, companies, institutions, and agencies need both effective management and ongoing leadership.

Management

Effective managers coordinate and facilitate all the business and organizational elements of Model A. They make things happen; but they make things happen through others. As managers of people, they make sure workers know what is expected of them, create clear paths to goals, provide resources and support, give feedback, monitor progress, and reward performance.

Leadership

Leadership is an interactive *process* involving the leader, team members or associates, and changing situations. Leadership goes beyond mere management to innovation and change. Leadership can be found at all levels:

- Executive
- Managerial
- Supervisory
- Professional/Technical
- Operational

Effective leadership is not predicated on the *traits* of the leader but rather on what he or she actually *accomplishes*. Leadership means (a) developing visions, (b) turning visions into workable agendas, (c) communicating these agendas to others in a way that results in excitement about and commitment to them, (d) creating a climate and ferment of problem solving and learning around the agendas, and (e) making sure that everyone persists until the agendas are actually accomplished. Leadership, in this sense, is at the heart of the search for excellence.

IV. Managing the Shadow Side of the Organization

The topic of managing the shadow side is not covered in this book. The author plans to make it the subject of a separate book at a later date. Nevertheless, it is so important that it needs to be mentioned briefly at this point. The shadow side of an organization includes the arational factors that affect both the business and organizational dimensions of the system. Wise managers know how to deal with the following elements:

• **The Natural Messiness of Organizations.** Organizations are loosely coupled systems in which the kinds of rationality outlined in Sections I, II, and III are only approximated. For instance, strategy and operations are not always well integrated.

• **Individual Differences.** Individuals working within systems have their differences, idiosyncrasies, and problems, all of which need to be addressed and managed. Research shows that people in leadership positions often imprint their traits, good or bad, on the organization.

• **The Organization as a Social System.** Organizations are social systems with all the benefits and drawbacks of such systems. Internal relationships and cliques develop that can help or hinder the business of the system.

• **The Organization as a Political System.** Because most organizations must deal with scarce resources and differences in ideology, they are political systems. Some people put self-interest ahead of the business agendas of the company or institution.

• **Organizational Culture.** Organizations tend to develop their own cultures and subcultures. The shared beliefs, values, and assumptions in an organization can either enhance or limit the system's effectiveness. The culture is the largest and most controlling of the systems, because it sets norms for what may or may not be done in all the other "shadow-side" areas.

The ability to manage the shadow side of the organization often makes the difference between a successful or unsuccessful manager or between a mediocre and an excellent manager.

Provisions of Model A

Model A is a business and organizational effectiveness model. It provides the following:

- An integrative framework for understanding companies, institutions, and their subunits.
- A template for designing and running a system.
- An instrument for assessing the effectiveness of a system and for choosing remedial interventions.
- A common language for talking about systems.
- A map for helping people to understand the *geography* of systems and to make their way around in them.

EXCELLENCE

In trying to determine precisely what makes a company or institution excellent, we find that some basics apply to all companies and institutions. Model A systematically outlines these basics. However, each system needs to tailor the basics to its own needs. Various authors and consultants suggest different formulas for excellence. For instance, Peters and Waterman (1982) listed eight norms, each of which relates to one or more of the four categories of Model A. Those eight norms, in essence, are as follows:

- Develop a bias for action rather than a bias for endless analysis.
- Stick close to your customers.
- Develop automony and entrepreneurship within the company or institution.
- Increase productivity by using the abilities of all employees.

- Establish business values and run the business according to them.

- Stick to your knitting, that is, stay in the business that you know best.

- Keep a simple structure and a lean staff.

- Determine what is important and what is not, then pursue the former with a vengeance.

Peters and Austin (1985) provide a formula that includes superior customer service, constant innovation, and full use of all the abilities of all the employees tied together by "management by wandering around." It is up to a given company, institution, or work unit to determine precisely which package of basics needs most attention. An application of the *Pareto Principle* (Zemke, 1986b) states, in managerial terms, that 80 percent of the results achieved by managers can be attributed to about 20 percent of the things they do. The trick, of course, is to discover which 20 percent will yield the 80 percent.

Figure 1-2 indicates how each of the areas of Model A can contribute to the ongoing *pursuit* of excellence, which is the hallmark of many successful enterprises in both the for-profit and not-for-profit sectors. The sequence of steps indicates the logic of Model A rather than a *time* sequence.

The following questions can provide some initial focus on what your company, agency, institution, or unit needs to do to pursue excellence:

- How excellent is our company or institution?

- To what degree are the basics outlined in this chapter in place in our system?

- What package do we need to develop to become an exemplar in our field?

- What is our formula?

The purpose of this book is to help answer those questions. Designing excellence principles of business and human resources into a new company, institution, or unit is often easier than changing the way an existing one operates. Some companies have adopted the strategy of building Model-A principles into new units before attempting to change the principles in operation in the older units. Once the new unit is up and running, it becomes a blueprint or exemplar unit for the other parts of the company. Work parties from other units visit or actually work in the new unit and experience the new approach firsthand. Challenged by this experience, they return to other units to stimulate changes there. This strategy has also been used by human-service institutions, as the following example indicates:

EXAMPLE: One order of nuns, committed to "staying on the cutting edge of secondary education in the United States," established an experimental high school in which educational innovation was the order of the day. The mission of this school was not just to educate its students. It included two other goals: to serve as a laboratory for the other schools operated by the religious community and to take its place—among other similar schools—as a center for experimentation and innovation in secondary education.

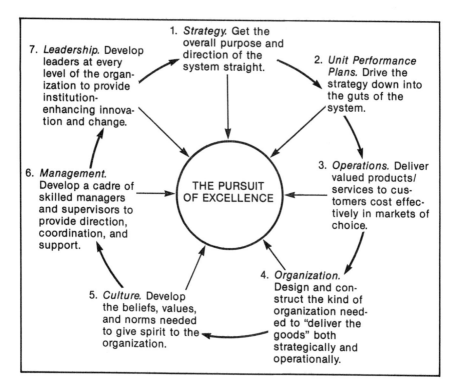

Figure 1-2. The Logic of the Pursuit of Excellence

As Peters (1987) suggests, excellence is not a destination, but rather a continual pursuit. Excellence is a question of degree, of will, of resources. Wise leaders will be able to adapt the simplified—and perhaps overly rational—suggestions in this book to the complex, arational realities of their companies and institutions.

PART I

BUSINESS DIMENSIONS

I-A. The Strategic Business Dimensions

I-B. The Operational Business Dimensions

In Part I the focus is on the business dimensions of the company, institution, or agency. Although in practice they are intimately related, it is helpful to make a distinction between the *strategic* and *operational* dimensions of any enterprise. Strategy focuses on overall direction. Who are we? What do we stand for? Where are we headed? What factors must we consider in setting goals for ourselves? Strategy deals with the longer-term viability of the system.

While strategy deals with direction and mandate, operations deals with the yearly, monthly, weekly, and daily fulfillment of this mandate. Operations deals with the actual design and the day-by-day delivery of products and services to customers. Operations, as Carlzon (1987) suggests, focuses on the enterprise's "moments of truth." If the system does not consistently deliver the products and services that customers need and want—if it fails during these moments of truth—then it is not fulfilling its mandate. Enterprises that fail to "deliver the goods" do not automatically disappear from the face of the earth. Many systems limp along in mediocrity and can do so because there are many other mediocre systems. This is especially the case with some human-service enterprises. For instance, the status of some school systems across the United States is more than distressing. Major corporations are discovering that they have to teach an increasing number of workers basic skills, including counting! There are at least two reasons for this. First, as we move more deeply into the Information Age, cognitive rather than merely manual skills become more and more important. Second, our educational systems fail to teach these skills to a significant number of students. The reasons why schools fail are complex. They relate to the schools themselves and to the demographic, economic, social, and professional realities in which school systems float. Whatever the complexity of causes, many schools when it comes to the delivery point—operations—simply do not or cannot deliver.

PART I-A

THE STRATEGIC
BUSINESS DIMENSIONS

Markets, Clients, Customers

Managing the Business Environment

Mission and Business Values

Establishing Major Categories

of Products and Services

Strategy

Surveys (Pearce & David, 1987) indicate that many businesses and institutions pay relatively little attention to the future and to strategic planning, even though a number of studies show that firms that do pay attention outperform firms that do not. Short-term rather than long-term considerations drive operations. However, the more turbulent the environment becomes in terms of the pace of business, technological, social, economic, and political change both here and abroad, the greater the necessity to consider strategic realities.

We live in an age in which the unthinkable has happened. Corporate giants that we once thought might go on forever have faltered and failed. International Harvester has had to eat humble pie. E.F. Hutton has been gobbled up. Many people believe that General Motors is in trouble. Steel companies are going under, downsizing, or fleeing to other businesses. Everyone knows that many of our school systems are in trouble, but no one has an easy remedy. Some business leaders of Pacific Rim countries are claiming that the day is coming when Europe will be their boutique, Australia their mines, and North America their granary. The Big Three automotive companies are facing the day when people will talk about the Big Twenty. Religions are taking on political roles worldwide. Years ago the late Marshall McLuhan (1964) announced the arrival of the "global village." Although his ideas seemed to be revolutionary at the time, in retrospect they seem tame.

Part I-A deals with strategic business issues. A whole range of questions arise. Are we focusing on the right markets? Do we understand the needs and wants of our customers in these markets? Do we have the right mix of products and/or services for our customers? Are we aware of both threats and opportunities in the environment and are we managing them well? Do we have a clear understanding of why we exist? Do we have a clear set of both ethical and business values that can serve as criteria for decision making? Do we know who we are and where we want to go? Do we enjoy the kind of financial health that will enable us to go where we like? There is no single correct strategic formula. Each enterprise must do the kinds of scrutiny and analysis that enable it to answer these questions. The more turbulent the environment, the more frequently must these questions be asked. Chapters 2 through 6 can help those who manage both entire systems and the subunits within those systems answer these questions.

2

Markets, Clients, Customers

The two major concerns of any business are (1) markets and customers and (2) products and services. Since companies, institutions, and communities are established to satisfy the needs and wants of customers, clients, and members, a logical starting point for Model A is markets and the needs and wants of consumers within those markets. The central business question is not "Do we have a product or a service to retail?" but rather "Are there markets and customers that need and want our products and services?" or "Is our product or service so good that it will create its own markets?" Many new restaurants fail each year because there is no market for what they have to offer.

DEVELOPING A MARKET MENTALITY

Markets can be either internal or external to the company or institution. In its widest sense, marketing includes factors such as the following:

- Market research data base; market niche; market growth rate; and market share.
- Customer needs and customer base.
- Product/service mix; completeness of product/service line; and product/service quality.
- Size and effectiveness of sales force; sales training; and selling expense.
- Advertising; the advertising budget; and advertising effectiveness.

- Warehousing; inventory levels; cost and quality of distribution; and prompt delivery.
- Customer service and customer satisfaction.

This section focuses on the need for a market mentality, that is, on an understanding of marketing in the widest sense and of the needs and wants of customers and clients in the market.

External Markets

A market can be a geographical area in which there is a demand for commodities or services. In this sense, automobile manufacturers talk about the Chicago market or the Denver market. A market can also be a group of people, however geographically distributed, with a common need or want. For instance, there is a ready market for drugs that could prevent, control, or cure AIDS.

During a four-day workshop on Models A and B in Dublin, I knew from scanning the registration forms that my audience included a number of submarkets—people from businesses such as manufacturing, insurance, and airport services; people from a variety of health-care systems, such as hospitals and clinics; people from different church settings; and people from educational institutions. Therefore, the services offered at the workshop needed to be presented in a way that would meet the needs of each of these markets.

Conn (1986) notes that lack of marketing knowledge on the part of entrepreneurs is the most common weakness cited by investors when they turn down opportunities to participate in start-up and early-stage companies, even when they themselves are willing to purchase the product the entrepreneur is offering. Investors want to know whether *others* want the product or service, and they want to know whether markets can be developed. Therefore, an understanding of markets and of the needs and wants of customers in the markets is the first order of business. Knowing which markets are in place and which need to be developed is essential. Failing to do market research or misreading markets is not the prerogative of would-be restaurateurs. A symbol of misreading markets is the Edsel, an automobile manufactured by Ford in the Fifties. The product was good enough in itself, but it found no real market niche and few customers. It proved to be a multimillion-dollar market mistake.

Throughout this book, examples will be taken from an airline company, which we will call "ABC Airways." ABC is a composite airline. The examples are drawn from a number of different companies in the industry.

EXAMPLE: ABC Airways, reading the rather turbulent environment for international travel, determined that market segmentation made more sense than trying to fly everywhere in the world. ABC tried to find answers to the following questions: In which markets do we excel? Which markets are better left to others? Which new markets are ready to be cultivated? Can markets be developed cooperatively with other airlines? Everything indicated that the Pacific Basin market, both business and leisure, would grow rapidly in the near future and that this should become a market of choice for ABC.

Developing a market mentality is useful for all companies and institutions. Questions such as "What kinds of needs and wants that we could meet are out there?" and "How extensive is the market?" can be asked by educational systems as well as computer companies. Just as I did some very "quick-and-dirty" market research for a conference in Dublin, so can teachers do the same for classrooms. Just like the diversity of markets represented in Dublin, classrooms are not usually homogeneous. They are composed of the motivated, the disinterested, the troubled, the slow learners, and the fast learners. Understanding such "markets" can help teachers deliver educational services that are tailored to actual needs.

The failure to take market realities into consideration backfired for a social-agency hotline. People with the best intentions started a hotline for abused children. The effort was launched on a national television program. The lines were deluged with calls. No one had any idea of the size of the market out there. Had they quietly tested the market in one part of the country, they might have avoided the organizational chaos and guilt, not to mention the infighting and politics, that ensued. They quickly hired staff to handle the avalanche of calls and just as quickly decided that they had hired the wrong people. They then selected volunteers while staff members were arguing about the feasibility of using volunteers. All in all, they were at a complete loss as to how to train both professional staff and volunteers for such a new venture.

Internal Markets

An understanding of markets is important even when the markets are internal to the company or institution. Large companies and institutions can have a number of different markets within them.

EXAMPLE: The head of the new management-development program at ABC Airways had a vision of a top-quality management training program that would challenge and change the management culture of the institution, help managers utilize its people more humanely and efficiently, and give them the kind of organizational expertise that would support more effective pursuit of business outcomes. Once the program in its broad outlines was cleared by the management committee, the head of the program had to determine where to start. By canvassing the senior managers of the institution, he learned that—although many of them gave either lip service or mild support to the program—they were not ready to dive in themselves. That is, the senior managers did not comprise his immediate market. The program head turned his attention to middle managers and eventually elected to start with relatively new managers, those who had been managers for six to twelve months. Interviews indicated that their needs were the most deeply felt. He then carefully chose and trained the first group of new middle managers. All of these were professionals and specialists in their own areas but knew relatively little about the art of management. Although many of them began the program with a great deal of skepticism, by the end of the program all of them enthusiastically endorsed it and began selling it to their colleagues. When the number of the middle managers moving through the program reached a critical mass, the program head turned his attention to senior managers, his most crucial market. The senior managers proved to be even more enthusiastic and open to learning than were their subordinates. They had been softened up by the staff members who had completed the program.

In organizations with a number of internal units, developing an internal-market mentality can help productivity. In one company, the new director of the accounting department soon realized that his department had a number of data bases that could provide the foundation for a range of new cost-reduction services throughout the company. He began a marketing campaign to sell these services.

ASSESSING THE NEEDS AND WANTS
OF CUSTOMERS IN MARKETS OF CHOICE

Companies and institutions exist in order to satisfy the needs and wants of markets and clients. Therefore, excellent companies develop whatever market- and customer-assessment instruments are necessary to identify the relevant needs and wants of the members of the markets of choice. These instruments include interviews, surveys, observations, research data, and intuition. Assessing needs and wants entails a data-gathering process. Of course, organizations gather data for a variety of reasons, and needs assessment is just one of the reasons. The following process, which can apply to any kind of data-gathering a company might do, is adapted from one suggested by Kilburg (1978). The focus here, however, is on the customer or client needs assessment. After each step of the process, an example of what ABC Airways would do is given.

1. **Clear Goals.** Determine what is to be accomplished through the data-gathering process; make sure the goal is concrete and clear. Avoid gathering data just for the sake of gathering data. Ask the following questions: Why is the data being gathered? How will it be used? To what decision does it relate?

ABC Airways would answer these questions in the following way: ABC wants to develop its business class on its international routes. The marketing department needs data in order to make decisions on establishing services that will attract and keep business travelers.

2. **Clear and Relevant Questions.** Formulate clear questions that will provide goal-related data. ABC wants to know what kind of amenities influence business travelers to choose one airline over another. The company also wants to know what business travelers like and dislike about its current business-class service.

3. **Appropriate Data-Gathering Instruments.** Determine what kind of data-gathering instruments seem to fit the situation best. Observations, interviews, questionnaires, surveys, and data from other companies are common techniques.

The observations of ABC flight attendants in the business sections of the aircraft are important sources of data. A study of the factors that seem to contribute to the success of business-class business in other airlines is launched.

4. Adequate Sampling. Use the instruments either with all the members of the system in question or with a representative sample.

ABC chooses to have as many business passengers as possible to complete in-flight questionnaires. ABC also decides to interview business passengers who are waiting in the departure lounge before flights and in the baggage pick-up area after flights. However, great care is taken not to become a nuisance in conducting these interviews.

5. Meaningful Data Analysis. Through analysis and interpretation, turn the data into information that is directly related to the decisions that need to be made.

If more than 50 percent of the business travelers surveyed express interest in a certain amenity—such as special baggage-handling services—ABC will give it immediate consideration.

6. Clear and Relevant Presentation of Results. Present the results in a form that can be understood as easily as possible by those who will review the data and/or make decisions based on the data.

The business travelers' request for special baggage-handling services is presented in graphic form to the director of marketing and the director of operations. They need to put their heads together and decide what type of baggage-handling services for business travelers makes sense for both marketing and operations.

7. Informed Decisions. Make decisions on the basis of this reliable and valid information.

ABC, on the basis of its research, provides special lounges for international business travelers. These lounges have work areas, computers, and plenty of telephones.

The assessment of needs and wants relates to both external and internal customers.

External Customers

A company or institution must assess the relevant needs and wants of the consumer of its products or services in its markets of choice. It must determine what the customers need and what they want.

> EXAMPLE: ABC Airways also did a great deal of research on the needs and wants of domestic business travelers because this, too, is a very lucrative market. The central question was "What has to be done to attract business travelers and ensure repeat business from them?" ABC discovered that these travelers wanted special treatment in making and revising reservations, in managing baggage, in boarding, and in seating. They also wanted convenient scheduling, on-time operation, room on the plane to do some work, minimum distractions, simple but high-quality food, and other amenities such as in-flight telephone service.

Identifying customer needs and wants is as important in human-service settings as it is in business. Like less-than-excellent companies, some not-for-profit institutions such as schools, churches, and service agencies fail to stay in touch with their markets and the needs of their customers within those markets. Then they wonder why they become marginal to the lives of the people they serve.

One of the cases in a film based on *In Search of Excellence* (Peters & Waterman, 1982) and presented on PBS was Leonard's Dairy, a supermarket that started as a family-owned dairy and grew by leaps and bounds because of its customer-oriented philosophy. Although an "ordinary" supermarket with 16,000 items was taking in about $200,000 per week at the time of the film, Leonard's was taking in $1,500,000 per week with 750 items. Like other stores, Leonard's provided excellent merchandise at a reasonable price. Unlike other stores, however, Leonard's was engaged in ongoing market research. Its staff listened to customers carefully and then acted on what was heard. Every second week volunteers among customers made up a "focus" group in which they discussed what they liked and did not like about the store. An oversized suggestion box highlighted by a large sign was emptied daily, and its contents were scrutinized. Input from the box was typed and circulated among the employees. Customers continued to volunteer for the focus groups because the store reacted to the feedback.

Internal Customers

Employees in an organizational unit whose immediate customers are internal (e.g., the accounting or personnel department or a research-and-development unit) often fail to develop a feeling for and an understanding of their clients. A financial unit produces reports, not for the soundness of the reports per se, but as decision-making resources for managers who constitute the clients of the unit. It is healthy for all units with internal customers to identify their flesh-and-blood clients and stay in touch with their actual needs. This would reduce the mountains of unused reports that managers in most organizations complain of. Units with internal customers should find answers to the following questions:

- Who are the people who receive my work?
- What do they need from me?
- How can I give them what is needed?

The key to the motivation of every employee—and the first step in involving everyone in attaining quality—is making sure that every employee has well-defined customers. If the definition of customer is expanded to include internal customers or clients, the contribution possible from each person becomes clearer. In the words of Townsend (1986):[1]

> [The customer is not just] the ultimate person or firm who actually buys and uses the firm's product or service; the customer is anyone to whom an individual provides any information, product, or service.... A particular worker's primary customer may very well be the person at the next desk or work station. The ultimate customers inhabit the outside world with money in their pockets; but the customers that the employee can do something about, those the employee can get immediate feedback from, may share the same roof.... Juran (1985) proposes that each person within an organization is a user, a processor, and a supplier. Each is a user, or customer, by virtue of being the recipient of a product, a service, or information in some incomplete stage of development. The role of processor may be taken

---

[1]From *Commit to Quality* (pp. 21-22) by P. L. Townsend, 1986, New York: John Wiley. Copyright 1986 by John Wiley. Reprinted with permission.

on by causing some physical change, by the adjustment of some data, or by the addition of a valued opinion. Having completed the processing (an act that may take seconds or weeks), the hat of supplier is donned, and the product, service, or information is passed along to a new user, or customer. For success, the varying standards of all customers must be met. (pp. 21-22)

For some organizations the very identification of and communication with internal clients would constitute a revolution.

The following questions are designed to help you assess the wants and needs of both internal and external customers and clients.

- How well do we do our market research with respect to external markets? With respect to internal markets?

- How well do we understand our external markets? Our internal markets?

- How well do we understand our clients and customers in these markets?

- How thoroughly are the needs and wants of customers in these markets identified?

- How well do we use the information that comes from formal and informal customer-needs assessments? What differences do the data make?

- How clearly are customers or clients and their needs distinguished from the needs and wants of other stakeholders, such as stockholders, managers, and directors?

3

Managing the
Business Environment

Every company, institution, and community has an environment. That is, each is surrounded and affected by other companies, institutions, and communities and by economic, social, and political conditions and events. External markets and customers, of course, are the central realities in the environment, but they are certainly not the only critical realities. The environment is the soup, and the veggies that float in it are the markets/clients/customers and the companies and institutions that serve their needs. Understanding and managing *externalities*—that is, the relationship between the company, institution, or community and the systems, individuals, and events with which it interacts and by which it is affected—are major tasks.

EXAMPLE: The administrator of a boys' reformatory wanted desperately to change the school for the better, but he did not know where to turn for help. Finally he happened to find a group of consultants who helped him totally change the school. A new mission was developed in which rehabilitation was central, and clear goals were established for administrators, guards, teachers, and inmates. The best guards were trained in helping and human relations skills, and they in turn trained other guards. Within a year one of the major outcomes—a dramatic drop in recidivism—was achieved. Then the total project was abandoned!

The administrator and the consultants had not monitored the political environment carefully. First of all, in the course of the change, some of the administrative team and some of the guards had been alienated. They complained to friends who were in a position to talk to people in power. Second, people higher up in the correctional system had not been brought on board, so they were unable to take any of the credit for the results. The venture ended with a futile encounter between the principal consultant and the governor. Politics won. The boys lost. The community lost. (See Carkhuff, 1974.)

If the environment is a highly politicized one, it needs to be factored into the management of the system. As Kanter (1983, p. 49) notes, "Management of critical boundary-spanning issues is a task of the top: developing strategies, tactics, and structural mechanism for functioning and triumphing in a turbulent and highly politicized environment." Threats, limitations, and opportunities abound; companies and institutions pursuing excellence know how to identify and deal with all three.

THE GENERAL ENVIRONMENT VERSUS THE SPECIFIC

As Hall (1972) indicated, there are differences between general and specific organizational environments.

The General Environment

General environmental conditions are the kinds of conditions "out there" that can affect many different kinds of companies, institutions, and communities. The general environment includes what Roeber (1973) calls *emergent systems* or what could be called *emergent environmental conditions*. Many of them are of a social, economic, ecological, legal, political, and cultural nature. Included are urban decay, demographic changes, changing sexual mores, the emergence of various forms of radical and ultraconservative politics, the antinuclear movement, anti-industry sentiment, the general decline of confidence in professionals in many different fields, the drug culture, women's movements, gay movements, sharply increased international competition, the international debt crisis, declining productivity, proliferating international "hot spots," variations in mortgage interest rates, and the proliferation and the power of political interest groups. When these and a host of others first emerge, they are often seen as environmental noise and nothing more. The fact that much of this noise has developed into movements that have profoundly affected society points to the necessity of developing ways to distinguish between noise that indicates critical trends and noise that indicates fads.

In Miles' (1980, p. 195) words, "General environmental conditions may be thought of as those that are potentially relevant for the focal organization. Moreover, the organization is not typically in touch with these elements on a day-to-day basis, but must create special environmental scanning and monitoring activities to deal with them."

The focal organization may not even be aware of how it is being affected by these conditions, even though these conditions are already living within the system and controlling it in various ways. As important as general environmental conditions are, they are hard to get at; but in a world of turbulent environments, the ostrich position is proving untenable. Louis Rukeyser (1987) reports the concerns of William P. Dunk, a corporate advisor, in this regard:

> We see managements paying attention to the small stuff, not the big issues. We seem to be entering a year of micro-management, not mega-leadership. Managers are tinkering around, while the dollar roller coasters, the tax system turns inside out, domestic and international capital markets run out of control, and IBM stalls. This is called biding your time while the Titanic trembles. (p. 3)

Many systems become aware of threats in the environment only when it is too late to do anything about them. Religious orders have long known that a whole host of environmental conditions were contributing to their decline but seem to have ignored St. Ignatius's sage advice to "pray as if everything depended on God but work as if everything depended on yourself." Only recently has there been public debate on the economic fate of aging nuns, brothers, and priests.

Companies, institutions, and communities can, of course, obtain help in scrutinizing the general environment. Companies have been established to help organizations monitor relevant trends (Naisbitt, 1982). BrainReserve, established in 1974, produces forecasts of consumer trends and helps companies reposition failing products or develop new ones. Industry publications, newsletters, journals, and magazines routinely provide forcasts of various kinds. For instance, a *Fortune* economic forecast (Brownstein, 1987) suggested that inflation would worsen slightly but still remain in control, there would be little economic growth, and consumer spending would increase by about 2.5 percent. Nevertheless, since things change so quickly in turbulent environments, continual environmental scanning is essential for some companies and institutions. The *Fortune* forecast on inflation was contingent on a steady dollar, but a few weeks after the forecast, trade sanctions were imposed on Japan, the dollar plunged to its lowest level against the yen, and financial markets were thrown into turmoil. A few months later the stock market crashed. It is not easy to keep track of the conditions in the general environment that might significantly affect any given company or institution, but it is becoming more and more necessary to try to do so.

The Specific Environment

The specific environments of companies, institutions, or communities are those other companies, institutions, and communities with which they are in direct contact and which are seen as having some kind of immediate or direct influence. Any given system can draw up a chart that indicates not only the companies, institutions, and communities that constitute its specific environment, but also the frequency of these contacts. Figure 3-1 charts the specific environment for a police department. This chart could be expanded to include the various neighborhoods or sections of the town and the frequency of incidents demanding police attention in each. The value of such an expanded chart can be immediately appreciated, because the department could, at a glance, obtain a view of both resources and demands placed on its services.

EXAMPLE: For ABC Airways, competitors form an important part of the specific environment. ABC, like many other airlines, offered air-freight service, and it wanted to determine whether or not to try to carve out a larger niche in that business. The decision-making process included a thorough exploration of the competitive environment. The study revealed seven high-capacity nonpassenger freight carriers. However, competition among them was intense, and it was likely that only three or four would survive the coming year. One of these was surviving only because of deep wage cuts and work-rule changes. This freight carrier might leave the domestic market and concentrate on the Pacific. Another, battered by losses, was looking for some kind of friendly takeover. A third one was the object of a hostile takeover by an Australian Company, and a fourth might also be a takeover target.

The industry's main issue was overcapacity. Other passenger airlines were once more courting freight business, which was up by 12 percent for the first six months of the year. To cap things off, the

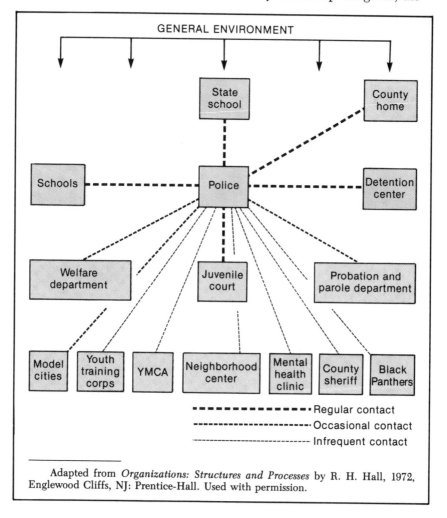

GENERAL ENVIRONMENT

State school

County home

Schools — Police — Detention center

Welfare department

Juvenile court

Probation and parole department

Model cities | Youth training corps | YMCA | Neighborhood center | Mental health clinic | County sheriff | Black Panthers

■ ■ ■ ■ ■ ■ ■ ■ ■ ■ ■ ■ ■ ■ Regular contact
-------------------------- Occasional contact
-------------------------- Infrequent contact

Adapted from *Organizations: Structures and Processes* by R. H. Hall, 1972, Englewood Cliffs, NJ: Prentice-Hall. Used with permission.

Figure 3-1. The Specific Environment of a Police Department

industry powerhouse, Federal Express, unexpectedly announced a price cut—a move that could start an industry-wide price war. (See "Airfreight Carriers," 1986, and "Federal Express Delivers," 1987.)

In view of all this, ABC decided to push its international freight business and adopt a wait-and-see posture in the domestic market. Like ABC, all companies and institutions need to keep monitoring the specific environment for events, trends, and movements that might spell opportunity or danger.

Interpenetration of System and Environment

What has been said thus far implies that systems are distinct from the environments that surround them. In a way this is not the case. The argument of Meyer and his associates (Meyer, et al., 1978) is that companies, institutions, and communities do not merely interface with their environments. Rather they are permeated throughout by their environments. Through their influence, outside systems live within and in very real ways construct and control the system in question. Take, for example, educational institutions; although they are sometimes seen as isolated from and even irrelevant to the society of which they are a part, this is not the case at all. As Reynolds (1982) expressed it:

> The connection between education and the workplace, school, and industry, is not in doubt. The design of curricula and scope of examinations are influenced by perceptions of future occupational or professional requirements. Leaders of industry and commerce are represented on the governing bodies of the institutions responsible for promoting educational research and teacher training. There is a constant pressure for education at all levels to be relevant to the needs of the workplace as defined by management. (p. 30)

The fact that both government and industry support research in universities opens channels of both direct and indirect influence. This, however, does not imply that such influence need be pernicious; it is mentioned because the topic is seldom publicly discussed.

MANAGING THE ENVIRONMENT

Change agents, whether internal or external, need to develop an *ecological* perspective. This requires the following three actions:

1. Scanning the environment and charting the principal systems and trends in the environment that are affecting or likely to affect the focal system.
2. Identifying opportunities and threats that need immediate attention.
3. Developing and implementing strategies for dealing with them.

Scanning and Charting the Environment

In *The Music Man* (the musical), salesmen are urged to "know the territory." For our purposes, the song would go "Ya gotta know the *environmental* territory." Environmental scanning is a process by which a focal system reviews systems and events in the environment with a view to maximizing the use of environmental resources and minimizing environmental risks. Metcalf, Riffle, and Seabury (1981, p. 4) define environmental scanning as "an iterative process to monitor events external to the [system]. . . a threat/opportunity screen to provide timely detection of changes significant to the [system]." Miles (1980, p. 322) defines scanning as "primarily a search for major discontinuities in the external environment that might provide opportunities or constraints to the organization."

An environmental chart identifies the individuals, systems, or trends in the environment that are significant for the system in question. Health-care systems have been barraged by changes in the environment—new government policies, increased sophistication of patients, the self-care and wellness movements, and competition. Currently, hospitals and clinics are diligently scanning both the general and specific environment for both threats and opportunities.

Choosing Threats or Opportunities for Attention

After identifying the key environmental systems and trends, the next step is to determine which individuals, systems, and/or trends are *critical* externalities; that is, which are most threatening and which are sources of the greatest opportunities. Any given externality may be critical in a *tactical* sense (i.e., it needs to be dealt with immediately), in an *operational* sense (i.e., it needs to be dealt with in the relatively short term, perhaps over the next year or two), or in a *strategic* sense (i.e., it has long-term significance and needs to be taken into consideration in the system's strategic planning).

> EXAMPLE: ABC Airways is thinking of entering the transatlantic market. Another airline is on the ropes and may be ready to sell its routes. This could be a strategic opportunity, or it could be merely a strategic temptation. Competition on these routes is fierce, and the market is easily disrupted by things such as terrorist attacks and unfavorable exchange rates. On the other hand, an opportunity like this might not come along again soon. ABC has to face the question, "What if a competitor snatches up the routes and uses them to feed passengers to its domestic routes in competition with ABC?"

Environmental scanning is too often implicit and reactive rather than explicit and proactive. Ideally it is an ordinary tool of an ongoing strategic planning process (see Chapter 6). However, if strategic planning is not a priority for the system, environmental scanning will not be, either.

Developing Action Plans
To Cope with Environmental Realities

Once significant environmental systems and trends are identified and the impact or potential impact is assessed, the next step is to plan strategies for taking advantage of opportunities and for managing or coping with threats. Systems need to adapt their coping strategies to changing environmental conditions. They must consider various factors—such as the importance of the decision being made, the degree of turbulence in the environment, and the degree of uncertainty remaining even after careful monitoring and scanning—and then decide whether action is called for. For example, health-care systems face turbulent environments, and reaction is not enough. They need to be proactive with respect to their set of externalities. Some elite clinics, including the venerable Mayo Clinic, provide a case in point. The following example is based on an article in *Business Week* (see "Even the Elite Clinics," 1987).

EXAMPLE: Mayo has drawn up a set of ambitious plans in order to thrive rather than merely survive in the new, hotly competitive, and cost-conscious health care market. In response to a prediction that ten to twenty SuperMed corporations will provide the bulk of the nation's health care by the decade of the Nineties, Mayo plans to merge with the two local hospitals to which it has been referring its patients and to build branch clinics in Florida and Arizona. Other prestigious clinics, such as the Cleveland Clinic, are moving in the same direction. Some are setting up their own HMOs to tap into the medical-insurance market lest they be left out by the SuperMeds. Dr. William S. Kiser, chairman of the Cleveland Clinic Foundation's board of governors, says, "Everybody must appeal to the consumer. Economic realities are driving the change." (p. 86)

Disturbed and turbulent environments place a great drain on the resources of systems. For instance, since certain information is at a premium in turbulent environments, a great deal of energy must be spent in intelligence operations. The efforts of ABC Airways to become a premier airline for business travelers in a highly competitive environment requires gathering a great deal of information, not only on the size of the market and of the needs and wants of business travelers, but also on what the competition is doing and intends to do.

A company facing a high-level threat or opportunity may resort to a set of strategies called "operations" by Emery and Trist (1965, p. 7), who define an operation as consisting of "a campaign involving a planned series of tactical initiatives, calculated reactions of others, and counteractions."

EXAMPLE: When Bendix tried to take over Martin Marietta in 1982, the latter borrowed a billion dollars and instituted a retaliatory takeover of Bendix. The strategy, however expensive, worked, but it forced Martin Marietta to sell off extraneous companies in order to focus on the aerospace business. This back-to-basics restructuring turned the company into a pared-down, cost-conscious operation long before this strategy became fashionable. However, executives at the company admit that they should have cleaned up their act without being forced to do so by Bendix. (See Moore, 1987.)

As of this writing, the leaner Marietta is doing quite well. Eventually, Bendix itself was acquired by Allied Corporation, and this acquisition put an end to the threat. Otherwise, Martin Marietta might have had to intensify its "operation."

LOOSE ENVIRONMENTAL COUPLING

To say that the environment often lives within and constructs the reality of any given system is not the same as saying that "everything is intimately related to everything else." Aldrich (1979) spells out the difference:

> Is it then plausible to assert that "everything is related to everything else"? If someone in New York sneezes, does someone in Peoria catch cold? Does the failure of the ABC Laundry in Boston affect the unemployment rate in Hartford? If the sociology department at Ivy University declines in prestige, does the chemistry department cease to attract qualified post-doctoral students?. . . There are countless examples, but the central point should be clear: Many situations in everyday life are only loosely related to one another, if at all, even within the same organization or group. (p. 76)

The important thing is not to assume that everything affects everything else or even to try to identify everything in the external environment that is having some kind of impact on the system. The key is to spot and deal with significant environmental opportunities and significant environmental threats.

A FINAL WORD

The following questions can help a system determine how excellent it is in terms of understanding and managing the environment.

- How proactive (as opposed to reactive) are we toward the environment?

- How well do we monitor the environmental trends that affect the way we do business?
- What individuals, systems, or trends are important or critical? In what ways?
- What environmental threats do we currently face?
- How well are we managing these threats?
- What unexploited opportunities have we identified in the environment?
- How well are we developing them?
- How time-sensitive are these externalities? How quickly do we have to act if we are to take advantage of a significant opportunity or fend off a significant threat?
- What environmental events or crises have taken us by surprise?
- What scanning procedures do we need to put in place when the environment is especially turbulent?
- To what degree do our findings about the environment affect our strategic direction?

4

Mission and Business Values

Markets and the needs and wants of customers within these markets constitute the starting point. The rest of Model A deals with providing products and services that can establish a market niche and satisfy the needs and wants of customers within the niche.

THE MISSION AND
THE MISSION STATEMENT

The *mission* is derived from and oriented toward markets and the needs and wants of cutomers within these markets. Mission deals with what the system is about, what its overall purpose is, what "business" it is in—whether it is a bank, a manufacturing concern, a church, a not-for-profit human-service institution, etc. Beckhard (1985, p.6) speaks of a "core mission" as "your *reason-to-be*, your sense of who you are as an organization" and adds, "A mission statement defines your reason-to-be as concisely and clearly as possible." The CEO (chief executive officer) of one large international bank stated its mission quite simply and concisely (and broadly!):

> The mission of the bank is to provide all financial services to every place in the world where it is legal and moral and on which we can make a profit.

Another bank worded its mission this way:

> The Mission of First Chicago Corporation is to be the premier bank in the Midwest with a reputation for excellence in serving customers nationwide and throughout the world.

It is more difficult for a conglomerate to state its mission concisely. The following paragraphs make up the mission statement of the Continental Group:

> From domestic packaging origins, Continental Group has become a diversified international corporation active in Packaging, Forest Products, Insurance, and Energy. Continental Group's primary function is to manage its resources to create wealth efficiently by producing and marketing quality products and services. While there will be many beneficiaries of this process—customers, employees, investors, suppliers, the society at large—success will ultimately be confirmed by producing a superior total return for shareholders. This can be done only by achieving sustained competitive excellence across the Company's operations.

A mission statement is easier to comprehend if the core mission is stated concisely before an explanation is given. ABC Airways, after agonizing over its mission statement for months, chose conciseness but added a particular slant:

> The mission of ABC Airways is to be the premier *service* company in all facets of the air-transportation industry. Moreover, ABC intends to be the world's best airline for business travelers in both domestic and international markets.

On the other hand, British Airways (BA), in its quest to become the world's "favorite" airline, issued a more discursive mission statement:[1]

> British Airways will have a corporate charisma such that everyone working for it will take pride in the company and see themselves as representing a highly successful worldwide organization.
>
> BA will be a creative enterprise, caring about its people and its customers.
>
> We will develop the kind of business capability which will make BA the envy of its competitors, to the enhancement of its stakeholders.

---

[1] British Airways Mission and Goals, issued April 1, 1986. Reprinted with permission of British Airways.

British Airways will be a formidable contender in all the fields it enters, as well as demonstrating a resourceful and flexible ability to earn high profits wherever it chooses to focus.

We will be seen as THE training ground for talented people in the field of service industries.

Whether in transport or in any of the travel or tourism activity areas, the term "British Airways" will be the ultimate symbol of creativity, value, service, and quality.

The BA statement can be summed up as "excellence in air transportation and all related travel tourism areas."

Communicating the Mission

It is critical that everyone in a company or institution understand and be driven by the central concepts and policies of the mission. General Motors executives carry around "culture cards" that spell out their new mission:

The fundamental purpose of General Motors is to provide products and services of such quality that our customers will receive superior value, our employees and business partners will share in our success, and our stockholders will receive a sustained, superior return on their investment.

Everyone in GM—not just the executives—should be a card carrier or, rather, a two-card carrier. One card should state in succinct, believable terms the mission of the overall system; the other should state crisply and clearly the mission of the *unit* in which the person works. One of Chrysler's truck plants pounded out the following mission statement:

We, the people of Dodge City, using our experience, knowledge, and pride, dedicate ourselves to being the world's finest truck builders.

The purpose of such a mission statement is to let everyone know that this plant is on the move, that it is going to be different. However, for such a mission to permeate the entire plant, each unit in the plant needs its own mission statement, one that is carefully linked to the overall mission of the plant.

The trick is to sink the mission into the consciousness of everyone in the company or institution. The common pitfall with respect to the mission, is that people at the top think—because they know what the mission is—that all employees know it. In many cases people on the line do not know it at all.

EXAMPLE: It makes little sense for ABC Airways to declare that it is in the service business if its employees do not have a service mentality. Ideally, each employee should be able to say, "We are first and foremost a service company." When ABC forged a new mission statement that gave voice to its aspiration to be a premier airline, the president of the company distributed to all employees a document that contained the mission plus his phrase-by-phrase commentary on it.

The manager of each unit in ABC was then charged with two things:
  1. To make sure that everyone in the unit understood the overall mission of the airline.
  2. To determine the mission of the unit and link that mission to the overall mission in a statement that could be understood by everyone in the unit.

The unit mission statement helps to guide day-to-day decisions in the unit. Effective managers and supervisors continue to develop strategies to keep the company mission and the unit mission fresh.

Refining the Mission Statement

The following questions, which relate to both a company or institution and its subunits, will help in developing appropriate mission statements and refining them.

- To what degree have we developed a realistic and forceful mission statement?
- How closely is this mission statement related to our markets and the needs and wants of customers within these markets?
- To what degree has this mission statement been communicated in practical ways to everyone in the system?
- To what degree is our mission statement a driving force for those working here?

- If there are conflicts over our mission, how are these conflicts managed?
- Do subunits have their own mission statements?
- To what degree are the mission statements of subunits integrated with our business mission?

BUSINESS VALUES AND POLICIES

The philosophy of a company or institution includes the beliefs, values, and norms or policies that drive behavior in that company or institution. A full statement of mission includes a clear statement of both central beliefs and cardinal values. In the chapter "Hands-On, Values-Driven," Peters and Waterman (1982) discuss how an explicit values orientation contributes to the success of companies and institutions. Regarding a request for "one truth" that could be distilled from excellent companies, they state:[2]

> We might be tempted to reply, "Figure out your value system. Decide what your company stands for. Put yourself out ten or twenty years in the future: what would you look back on with greatest pride?" We call the fifth attribute of the excellent companies, "hands-on, values-driven." We are struck by the explicit attention they pay to values, and by the way in which their leaders have created exciting environments through personal attention, persistence, and direct intervention—far down the line. (p. 279)

O'Toole (1985), in a study of "vanguard" companies, states that they both know and live their values. He discovered that they have four characteristics in common: They are fair in their dealings with all stakeholders, they are dedicated to high purpose with profit seen as a means rather than an end, they are committed to discovery and learning, and they strive to be the best at everything they do.

The value-based mission of Johnson & Johnson (Figure 4-1) is stated in terms of its responsibilities to various stakeholders. High language such as this needs to be translated into behavior in a system's

---

[2]Excerpt from *In Search of Excellence: Lessons from America's Best-Run Companies* by Thomas J. Peters & Robert H. Waterman, Jr. Copyright © 1982 by Thomas J. Peters & Robert H. Waterman, Jr. Reprinted by permission of Harper & Row, Publishers, Inc.

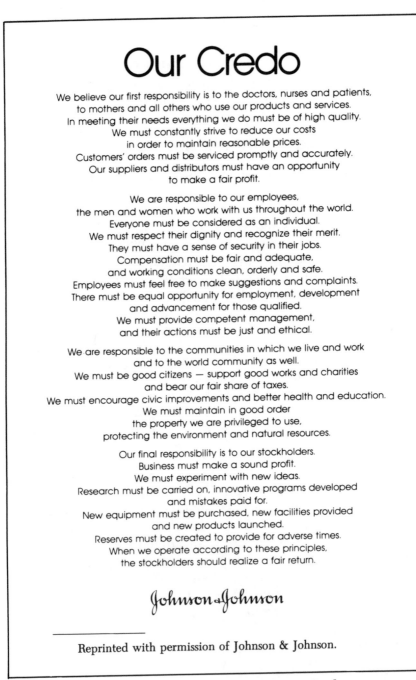

Our Credo

We believe our first responsibility is to the doctors, nurses and patients,
to mothers and all others who use our products and services.
In meeting their needs everything we do must be of high quality.
We must constantly strive to reduce our costs
in order to maintain reasonable prices.
Customers' orders must be serviced promptly and accurately.
Our suppliers and distributors must have an opportunity
to make a fair profit.

We are responsible to our employees,
the men and women who work with us throughout the world.
Everyone must be considered as an individual.
We must respect their dignity and recognize their merit.
They must have a sense of security in their jobs.
Compensation must be fair and adequate,
and working conditions clean, orderly and safe.
Employees must feel free to make suggestions and complaints.
There must be equal opportunity for employment, development
and advancement for those qualified.
We must provide competent management,
and their actions must be just and ethical.

We are responsible to the communities in which we live and work
and to the world community as well.
We must be good citizens — support good works and charities
and bear our fair share of taxes.
We must encourage civic improvements and better health and education.
We must maintain in good order
the property we are privileged to use,
protecting the environment and natural resources.

Our final responsibility is to our stockholders.
Business must make a sound profit.
We must experiment with new ideas.
Research must be carried on, innovative programs developed
and mistakes paid for.
New equipment must be purchased, new facilities provided
and new products launched.
Reserves must be created to provide for adverse times.
When we operate according to these principles,
the stockholders should realize a fair return.

Johnson & Johnson

Reprinted with permission of Johnson & Johnson.

Figure 4-1. The Johnson & Johnson Credo

dealings with its stakeholders. Johnson & Johnson did just that during the crises with the Tylenol capsules. Their public-relations people did not attempt to stonewall the issue. Rather, they were completely open with the media and the public. They used their CEO to reiterate the company's principles, which they stood by.

EXAMPLE: ABC Airways developed a "fair-deal" policy for customers that goes beyond governmental regulations. If a customer is dissatisfied, every effort is to be made to make things right. This general policy is concretized in such practices as helping passengers switch to earlier connecting flights on another airline if the late arrival of an ABC flight forces a passenger to miss a connection.

Perhaps the real test of the value system of a company or institution lies in its dealings with powerless stakeholders (e.g., little people, the poor, the disenfranchised) and the environment (e.g., refusing to dump toxic waste even when no one is looking). Companies, institutions, and communities—like individuals—do not always live up to their values. As Argyris (1982) puts it, espoused values are not always the values-in-use in any given system. Or, in O'Toole's (1985) words,

What is significant about the Vanguard corporations is that there is congruence between the values espoused in their constitutions and the actual practices of these corporations. In distinction, some Old Guard corporations have high-sounding constitutions, but there is a contradiction between rhetoric and performance that belies their noble words. (p. 52)

However, it is still better for a system to state its values explicitly so that the members of the system and those whom the system affects have explicit criteria for accountability. Then the system can be challenged in various ways from within and from without to live up to the values it espouses. The following questions can help a system focus on its business philosophy:

- To what degree do we have a coherent business philosophy, that is, a set of major beliefs, values, and policies, which permeate and guide our work?
- How clear is this philosophy to all who work here?
- How clearly has our philosophy been communicated to our clients or customers?

- To what degree is the way we operate consistent with our espoused philosophy?

A PEOPLE MISSION

People make things happen in companies and institutions. Although human resources are considered in Part II of Model A, it is essential right from the start to link productivity (i.e., the delivery of quality products and services in a cost-efficient way) to the kind of quality of work life (QWL) that goes hand in hand with and contributes to productivity. Quality of work life deals with the satisfaction of the legitimate needs and wants of workers in the work place. A worker-oriented mission statement needs to parallel the business mission statement. Better still, the overall mission statement should be integrated, that it, it should include policies that deal with both people and productivity—like the Johnson & Johnson "Credo" (see Figure 4-1).

One of Chrysler's plants came up with the following mission:

To be the first in world automotive assembly technology and quality, utilizing the latest concepts in employee participation/involvement, automation, and design techniques.

This at least moves toward an integrated mission statement, because it refers to the latest concepts in employee participation/involvement. A full, people mission statement specifies the general orientation of the company or institution to its human resources, establishes the values on which employee-related policies will be based, and identifies the major personnel policies that will govern the interactions between the company or institution and those who work in it.

EXAMPLE: ABC Airways is a nonunion carrier that has enjoyed excellent relationships between management and employees. Attempts to unionize ABC's workers have always been soundly defeated. Most employees are stockholders. One of ABC's major policies is not to lay off employees in times of economic downturn unless this is absolutely necessary in order to keep the company from going under. Employees may be asked to work reduced schedules, to take voluntary furloughs, to take early retirement, or to come up with other strategies that will help the company weather the storm. During one recession, the employees bought the airline a new plane.

When the deregulation of the airline industry led to nearly cut-throat competition—which in turn led to severe cost-cutting measures—ABC set up a cross-organizational task force to study the impact of the new competition. The task force also developed contingency proposals, which were based on ABC's people philosophy, for managing the fallout from deregulation.

Since QWL needs to be integrated with productivity from the very beginning, the need for a parallel people-related mission is clear. Only a small percent of QWL can be achieved through employee perks. A good estimate is that 80 percent of QWL must come from employees' efforts to do the work, to deliver the products or services, and to otherwise pursue company or institutional goals. The efforts are more likely if employees participate in decisions that affect their lives.

Model A does not deal with QWL as a separate issue or category, because QWL considerations need to permeate and be integrated with all elements of the model.

The relationship between productivity and QWL runs in both directions. For instance, if working conditions and wages are poor in a nursing home, then workers might well refuse to work up to their potential. Because they feel that they are being treated unfairly, they might even engage in subtle forms of sabotage. Then the quality of life of the customers—that is, the patients—also suffers. In this example, poor QWL affects productivity.

On the other hand, poor productivity can affect QWL. If an airline is reeling from the effects of deregulation, is being bashed by the competition, and is being considered by the financial community as a likely candidate for the trash heap or a takeover, its inability to meet business objectives can sour the work climate quickly. One critical hygienic factor, *security*, is on the line. One critical motivating factor, a sense of achievement, is also on the block. No one enjoys belonging to a loser.

Nevertheless, good working conditions do not automatically lead to increased productivity. Likewise, a well-run, productive company does not automatically create high worker morale. The fusion of the two is the important factor. If workers are well treated and if the company or institution is run well, then the odds are in favor of a good climate. Other things being equal, people will like going to work better and will be more productive while they are there.

A People Triangle

In summary, we can say that a company or institution needs a *people triangle*, in which each angle constitutes one of the following three interacting features:

Angle 1. A well-conceived human resources strategy, which is composed of an idea, a guiding concept, a rallying cry, or a gospel and a set of sound personnel policies that permeates the system and helps everyone in the system to focus on QWL issues.

Angle 2. Effective people managers and supervisors, who understand both the needs of workers and the productivity needs of the system and who know how to integrate both.

Angle 3. Employee-friendly systems. The physical facilities, policies, procedures, methods, and communication processes must say to all those who work in the system, "Everything here is designed to meet your legitimate needs as we strive for productivity."

The following questions will help in the search for excellence in the management of human resources:

- Do we have a coherent people mission?
- To what degree is this major statement concerning the quality of life of our employees integrated with our business mission?
- To what degree does this statement drive the behavior of the organization?
- To what degree have QWL policies been designed into our organization rather than added on?
- To what degree have subunits in the organization derived explicit people missions from the overall people mission of the company or institution?

Sticking to one's values in dealing with all stakeholders demands integrity. O'Toole (1985) translates integrity into behavior, suggesting that it lies in the moral courage to do tough things; for example, to resist pressures for short-term gains at the expense of long-term viability, to take unpopular but system-enhancing positions, to stick to one's values in hard times, or to hire people that are more capable than oneself. This is the right stuff of which excellence is made.

5

Establishing Major Categories of Products and Services

The core mission delineates the overall business of the system. It is, however, a generic statement that needs to be translated into major categories of products or services. In a sense, mission provides the vision, while the major categories of products and services constitute the principal agendas that flow from that vision, and the strategy outlines the game plan for adapting these agendas to the market place. This chapter considers the establishment of major categories of products and services, and Chapter 6 discusses strategy.

The following example illustrates how a company translates its mission into major categories.

EXAMPLE: Some of the major product categories of the Honda Corporation are automobiles, motorcycles, and small motor-driven products such as lawn mowers and emergency generators. Honda's Automotive Division has long been involved with the North American automobile market with an expanding range of automobiles carrying the Honda name. In terms of Model A, the mission of that division has been translated into three major categories of products: Honda Civics, Honda Accords, and Honda Preludes. A number of different products are also in these major categories.

Recently Honda decided to move into the luxury-car market to compete with European exports such as Mercedes and BMW. Honda's luxury-car division was given a new name: Acura. The car at the top of this line is the Acura Legend, and the Honda Corporation hopes to carve out a niche in the luxury market.

The logic of the process of translating mission into major categories of products or services is similar in all kinds of businesses, including church, educational, and human-service businesses. Once a market is identified and the needs and wants of customers in that market have been assessed, the company or institution develops a mission that establishes its purpose and identity. Then, basing its decision on a review of markets and customers, it determines precisely which set of market and client needs it will address and establishes major categories of products or services to meet these needs.

EXAMPLE: United Medical Corporation, when founded in 1972, provided cardiac-rehabilitation services on an outpatient basis. Over the years it added a variety of health-care business categories: operating kidney dialysis centers, testing the reliability of implanted pacemakers, providing test data to pharmaceutical companies, analyzing the results of twenty-four-hour electrocardiograms, distributing medical supplies, and manufacturing a line of exercise treadmills.

Major categories of service can be seen from two perspectives in ABC:

EXAMPLE: A holding company owns ABC Airways. This company also owns a chain of hotels and a car-rental firm. Air transportation, hotel service, and auto rentals are the three major categories of services offered by the holding company. Therefore, ABC *is* one of the major categories at that level.

ABC, in turn, has several major categories of services: scheduled flights (with economy, business, and first-class offerings), charter service, vacation packages (through a wholly owned holiday-tour subsidiary), a small-package express service, and air-freight services. The airline offers both domestic and international services in all these categories.

Like other businesses, ABC Airways must continually review its product categories in light of market and other environmental conditions.

EXAMPLE: The products offered by the tour division of ABC Airways are well known in North America, but few attempts have been made to interest European visitors in them. Since the value of many European currencies has appreciated against the U.S. dollar, many Europeans are considering tours to the U.S. Therefore, the ABC tour division sees an opportunity for developing its North American holiday-package business in the European market.

On the other hand, the small-package express business is languishing because of fierce competition. ABC is thinking that now may be the best time to eliminate that category.

Human-service agencies and institutions also develop major categories of services. For instance, a high school may decide that its mission (vision) is the holistic human development of its students and then formulate its major categories of services in terms of (a) academic competence, (b) social-emotional growth and development, (c) physical growth and development, and (4) values clarification and construction. These major categories carve out specific areas of student needs, and a range of services is provided in each major category.

A rape crisis center wanted to expand its function in the community. It had engaged almost exclusively in direct services to rape victims. However, many of the workers wanted to tackle rape as a social problem. Although they believed that the direct-service work was invaluable, they wanted to move into education and advocacy. Figure 5-1 indicates how they translated their new mission—helping both actual and potential victims of rape and challenging society to cope with rape more effectively—into additional service categories.

STICKING TO KNITTING

Peters and Waterman (1982) found that the best-run companies in the United States generally "stick to their knitting"; that is, they do not branch out into businesses they do not know how to run, nor do they add categories of products and services that distract them from their primary mission. Therefore, when the rape crisis center wanted to expand the categories of services it offered, it needed to make sure (a) that these services met real needs in the community, (b) that its staff members had the skills and resources to do so, and (c) that the new categories of services would not diminish the quality of those currently being provided. When one of the giant oil companies entered the office-automation business, it went outside the stick-to-your-knitting principle. Its antiquated word processor was a subject of humor at trade shows, and even the off-brand model

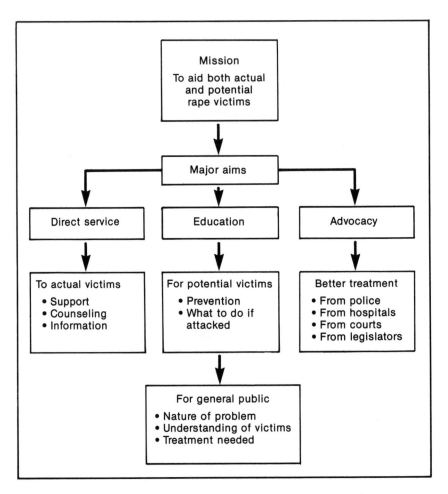

Figure 5-1. Expansion of Services by a Rape-Crisis Center

that replaced it failed to generate much excitement. Later the company dropped the office-automation business. Quaker Oats has based some recent divestiture decisions—notably its specialty retailing division—on the stick-to-your-knitting principle (Goodman, 1986):[1]

---

[1]From "Eyelab Sale Shows Why Quaker Nixed Specialty Retailing" by J. Goodman, 1986, *Crain's Chicago Business*, August 18-24, p. 1. Copyright 1986 by Crain Communications, Inc. Reprinted by permission.

Quaker Oats Co.'s decision to sell its specialty retailing group reflects the discomfort a giant in the food industry felt in attempting to manage a smaller, non-food enterprise. . . . Nowhere is that discomfort clearer than in the case of Eyelab, Inc., the division's smallest and most recent acquisition, and one that was heralded with high hopes when it was bought not quite three years ago. . . . Now, Eyelab is on the block, along with Jos. A. Bank Clothiers, Inc. and Brookstone Co. But it is Quaker's experience with the eyeglass superstore chain more than the others that explains the company's disaffection with specialty retailing, and its decision to devote greater attention to grocery products. . . . With Eyelab, Quaker found itself nurturing a brash young retailer trying to grow up quickly in a new industry that lacked established rules. (p. 1)

The culture at Quaker Oats stresses caution and quality control, whereas the new eyeglass superstore chains currently stress aggressive growth. The brashness needed for specialty retailing is foreign to Quaker Oats. Its experience in specialty retailing has enabled its officers to say, "This is not our kind of thing." The injunction "stick to your knitting" is not, on the other hand, meant to destroy initiative, creativity, or the entrepreneurial spirit. For instance, in the space of six years Kemper Corporation has transformed itself from a rather staid insurance company into a very profitable conglomerate in the area of financial services. Kemper has acquired regional brokers and has developed Kemper Financial Services, Inc. (see *Business Week*, September 8, 1986):

In four years [Kemper] has nearly doubled the mutual funds and other assets it manages to roughly $36 billion. The parent company also has large property-casualty and life insurance operations under its corporate umbrella. An expansion of its reinsurance business, which takes on part of another insurer's risk in return for premium income, has catapulted Kemper from 10th place to seventh among U.S. reinsurers in the past two years. . . . In life insurance. . . Kemper was one of the first to recognize public disenchantment with old-fashioned whole-life policies and to promote interest-rate-sensitive products. (p. 78)

What can be said of conglomerates such as Quaker Oats and Kemper can also be said of much smaller businesses, including not-for-profit agencies and institutions. For instance, if the members of a church ask themselves whether they should move into political advocacy, at least in areas affecting the fundamental beliefs and moral values for which the church stand, they need criteria to determine whether this makes sense or not, for they are adding or expanding a "product." One of the criteria is, obviously, the mission of the church. Another is the church's definition of who its members are and who the target groups of its mission are. As mentioned earlier, human-service institutions have—at least in an analogous sense— their markets and clients.

CARVING A NICHE

One of the ways in which a company or institution achieves a sense of identity is to carve out a niche for itself in the marketplace. As the following example shows, International Multifoods ("Multifoods is Ditching," 1986) has decided to do just that.

> EXAMPLE: International Multifoods had so many little businesses and so many different products that it did not know what it was. Now it has started to jettison some of its products (e.g., wheat germ, granola cereals, a cheese spread, and meat snacks) as well as two retail fish stores, the Boston Sea Party restaurant chain, a pet-food business, and thirty-one Hickory Farms cheese and sausage stores. International plans to concentrate on flour milling, bakery mixes, and animal feed—the businesses in which it is a top competitor. (p. 34)

Developing a niche is not the same as refusing to take risks or becoming staid and stale. Compaq Computer Company is currently choosing to carve out a niche in IBM's home territory. Its strategy is to provide a range of quality products together with the software to run them in advance of the computer giant. One way to develop the criteria for determining whether to add a major product or service category is to formulate a strategic plan. The following questions about principle agendas will help in determining major categories of products and services:

- What are the major areas in which we can deliver quality products and services?
- How do these categories relate to our overall mission?
- To what degree are these categories based on market research?

- Which categories should be dropped? Which should be added?
- What evidence do we have that we are sticking to our knitting?
- How effective have we been in carving out a niche in which we are known and respected for our quality products or services?

6

Strategy

A company or institution, in order to remain productive, needs to engage in many different kinds of planning. Three kinds are considered in this book:

1. Strategic planning
2. Unit performance planning
3. Individual performance planning

STRATEGIC PLANNING

The kind of planning that relates specifically to the mission and the establishment of major categories of products or services is called *strategic planning*. Clifford (1981) describes strategic planning as follows:

> [Strategic planning is] the capacity of an organization to deal with the long-term, fundamental requirements of the institution and its constituent businesses and to maintain a balance of these strategic considerations with inevitably intense pressure for short-term performance. (p. 1)

Nicholls (1981) offers another description:

> [Strategic planning is] the analytical and creative process whereby strategies are developed to cope with. . .competitive [environmental] forces or shape them to our advantage. It involves no more than thinking creatively about the business, the competition, and the forces of change at work in the environment to identify emerging opportunities and threats. (p. 3)

He also says that strategic planning is useless without strategic management, that is, "the ability to translate [plans] into realistic programs and objectives that can be implemented by all levels of the organization" (p. 5).

Pfeiffer, Goodstein, and Nolan (1986) give the following definition:

> Strategic planning is the process by which the guiding members of an organization envision its future and develop the necessary procedures and operations to achieve that future. (p. 1)

They also mention that strategic planning differs from mere long-range planning. Strategic planning, like long-range planning, deals with the long term. In long-range planning, however, the company starts with the present and extrapolates the future from present realities. A strategic plan, on the other hand, starts with a vision of the future and asks, "What do we need to do to get there?" Long-range planning makes sense in placid environments; strategic planning deals with turbulent environments. Sculley (1987) notes the differences and explains how strategic planning works at Apple:

> Most corporate planners decide where the company should go in the next year or two by peering into the company's past and making judgments and extrapolations based on their experiences. We ask ourselves, What will 1992 be like? We create in our minds a portrait of the economy, our industry, and our company. Then we move back into the present, envisioning what we have to do to get to the future. (p. 116)

Long term means different things to different companies or institutions. For some the business environment is so turbulent and volatile that two years might be a realistic long term. For others, five or ten years might be appropriate.

A strategic plan, at least in its basic form, deals with the following factors: the business mission, the major categories of products or services the business intends to provide, the markets and customers that constitute the targets of these products or services, the notion of market niche, the internal resources of the company or institution, and the relevant opportunities and threats posed by the environment. The answers to questions about each of these factors constitute the criteria for determining the business game plan. The following questions provide examples:

- In what ways does our mission need to be updated?
- In light of our mission, what major categories of products or services do we want to provide?
- Do we have what it takes to develop markets?
- How ready are existing markets to receive our products or services?
- Given current competition, can we carve a niche for ourselves in the marketplace?
- To what degree do we have the resources such as expertise and financing to manufacture and/or distribute these products or deliver these services?
- To be successful, what environmental opportunities do we need to take advantage of?
- To avoid failure, what environmental threats need to be managed?
- What degree of risk is involved in all of this and to what degree are we prepared to take risks?

Obviously, the questions need not be answered in the above order. Nevertheless, there is a dynamic interaction between markets, market niche, general and specific environmental threats and opportunities, mission, business values, major categories of products and services, and organizational resources. Strategy emerges from an analysis of all these factors.

Even though a strategic plan aims at the longer term, it needs to be reviewed and updated throughout the period it covers. At its best, it is a *living* instrument that adapts itself to internal and external realities. For instance, a company with a five-year strategic plan would do well to update its plan yearly or even more often if crises intervene. Fluctuations in oil prices have forced many oil companies to reformulate their strategic plans. Since the term "plans" often connotes something that is fixed, perhaps it is better to talk here about *strategy* or *direction* rather than a strategic plan. Strategies are living things that can be changed or adapted to unforeseen realities through tactics.

Although common sense may seem to dictate having a strategic plan, most companies and institutions have no such plan. Some think that strategic planning was a fad of the Seventies. Strategic planning, of course, can be a formality, and it can be unrealistic. Many times an elaborate plan is developed by people who have little to do with its implementation; then it lies unused—in all its elegance—in a drawer. In one company with which I worked strategic planning was relegated to a subunit in the personnel department. All sorts of reports were produced, but none seemed to influence strategy.

EXAMPLE: ABC Airways, having spent years without a strategic planning process, jumped on the bandwagon in the late Seventies and produced elaborate but meaningless plans. In the light of domestic deregulation, growing international competition, and an ongoing turbulent economic environment, ABC needed a more realistic game plan. An analysis of the airline industry and the economic environment in which it operates suggested that the bigger companies will remain viable. Therefore, ABC designed a strategy that included reasonable growth. First, ABC would establish mutually beneficial contracts with a series of commuter airlines. These airlines, while remaining independent companies, operate under the "ABC Express" logo, feed local passengers into ABC's domestic routes, and benefit from ABC's "aura" in terms of increased traffic. Second, although ABC saw some of the smaller domestic airlines as ripe for acquisition, it would avoid hostile takeovers lest it gain the reputation as the industry predator. Third, it saw the Pacific Basin as the most promising market for development and would enter negotiations with another major airline—which was currently a bit down on its luck—to purchase these routes. ABC decided on a three-year time frame for these elements of its strategy.

Too many businesses live from day to day; and then one day, much to their surprise, they discover they are no longer viable. Many human-service institutions—such as churches, schools, governmental agencies, and the helping professions—are hurt by their failure to keep up with social changes. Some churches, seeing themselves rooted in tradition and doctrine and supported irrevocably by God, do little to adapt themselves to the world as it is. For instance, in Great Britain, while fundamental religious values still persist, indifference to the established institutional church is massive. The medical industry has been racked by such factors as drastic changes in government funding, the continued development of expensive technology, and the oversupply of hospital beds. Both public and private institutions of higher learning face their own set of crises, including the possibility of reduced support because of imminent tax-reform legislation. In summary, meaningful strategic planning is no longer a curiosity or a luxury. Detailed step-by-step guides to creating a strategic plan are readily available (e.g., Mason & Mitroff, 1981; Pfeiffer, Goodstein, & Nolan, 1985, 1986; and Steiner, 1979).

The Business Plan

The term "business plan" can mean many things. Here it is defined as a *link* between the strategic and the operational dimensions of a company or institution. The business plan indicates how resources will be allocated to various units of the organization in the light of strategic objectives. For instance, if a company wants to become market driven, the business plan will allocate to marketing the kinds of resources needed to pursue its new mission.

Planning, whether strategic, operational, or individual, does not work some kind of productivity magic in the system. At its best it helps workers put order in things and it stimulates them to be more creative in their thinking. One of its most important functions is to stimulate communication among individuals and among organizational units. Planning at its best generates useful information, helps people analyze it, and disseminates it to those who can turn it into productivity.

The following questions will help you analyze the current state of strategic planning in your company or institution:

- How well does our planning stimulate creativity and foster productivity-centered communication?

- How skilled are our people in thinking strategically? That is, do they think about creating the future rather than waiting for it to happen?

- To what degree is strategic thinking blotted out by our day-to-day operations?

- What kind of strategic plan do we have?

- How well does our strategic plan integrate (a) market/client needs, major environmental factors, and our mission with (b) our business philosophy and values and (c) our choice of major categories of products and services?
- How often do we review and update our strategic plan?
- How well do we drive the strategy down into the guts of our company or institution?
- To what degree is there is a sense of strategic direction in our company or institution?

Figure 6-1 pulls the principal strategic dimensions together in graphic form. Each company or institution needs to do its own analysis, come to its own decisions, and establish its own priorities in each of these areas. The integration of all of them constitutes strategy or direction.

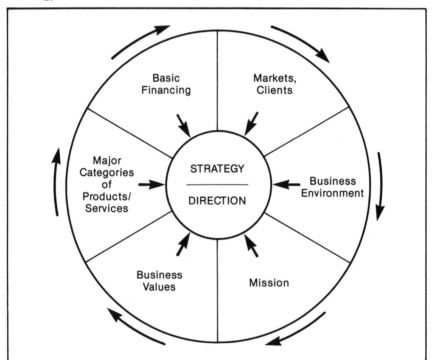

Figure 6-1. Strategic Business Dimensions: Factors Contributing to Strategy and Direction

PART I-B

THE OPERATIONAL BUSINESS DIMENSIONS

Products and Services

Work Programs

Managing Material Resources

Unit Performance Planning

Up to now, the strategic direction of the entire enterprise has been discussed. Strategy is meaningless unless it gets into the guts of the organization. That means that each unit within the organization has to deliver the goods. *Operations* refers to the delivery of specific products and services by each and every organizational unit to internal or external customers. The ABC flight crew delivers the actual flight to passengers, but a whole variety of units must deliver products or services before the flight takes place. For instance, catering has to deliver food to the plane so that meals can be served by the flight attendants. Fuel must be delivered before the plane can take off. Other units, such as reservations and departure-gate personnel, deliver services directly to customers in preparation for the flight. Each unit also has its own work programs, budget, and material resources. The unit performance plan pulls all this together and relates it to the overall strategy of the company or institution.

7

Products and Services

In each major category of products or services are the *specific* products and services that actually satisfy the needs and wants of customers. These products and services constitute the heart of the business of any company or institution. The sacred moment is the moment the satisfied customer drives his or her new Honda out of the dealer's premises or the time the passenger spends flying from LaGuardia to O'Hare on one of United's planes or the tasteful and moving liturgical ceremony in which a couple's new daughter is baptized. Ideally, any given product or service should be (a) of *value*, that is, satisfy some need or want at a reasonable price, (b) of high *quality*, and (c) accompanied by excellent customer service.

MEASURING WORTH: USEFULNESS AND PRICE

The *worth* of a product or service involves its value or usefulness and the ratio between its value and its price. If a product or service has little or no value or if the price is too high for its value, then it is not worthy.

Usefulness

Products and services have value only if they are perceived by clients or customers to meet relevant needs or wants. If a company has failed to do its market research well, even a high-quality product may prove to be a failure. Ford's Edsel may well have been a high-quality product, but it did not find a niche in the marketplace. Faulty market research was probably a principal factor in the failure of the Edsel. *Producing* an automobile is not enough; producing one that appeals to buyers is essential. Likewise, it is not enough for training departments of corporations to produce training events that help members of the sytem improve their skills; those skills must be relevant, that is, they must enable people to do their work more effectively and efficiently. It is not enough for a church to present just any kind of liturgy as an act of communal worship. The liturgy should capture the minds and hearts of the congregation so that they feel renewed in their desire to commit themselves to the mission of the church in their private and public lives.

Favorable Value-Price Ratio

A product or service is, in Gilbert's (1978) term, *worthy* if it is seen as useful by the customer or client and if its value outweighs the price to be paid. If parents pay a hundred thousand dollars for a series of operations to save their daughter's life, they see the operations as worthy, because the life of their daughter is valuable to them beyond price. On the other hand, a fifty-thousand-dollar automobile suffers from an unfavorable value-price ratio for many people who could afford it. Companies need to experiment to arrive at the right ratio, as illustrated in the following example.

EXAMPLE: In a marketing experiment, ABC Airways converted some of its wide-body planes from first and economy classes to business and economy classes. By using movable curtains and folding down middle seats to provide a table that would separate the passenger in seat A from the passenger in seat C, the crew could vary the size of the business-class section. The customers in the business section had more room, received a newspaper, and at times received warm meals while passengers in the economy section were receiving cold snacks. Since business-class passengers were in the front of the plane, they were able to get off first.

Business passengers valued these amenities, but the amenity-price ratio had to be right. ABC had to determine what price would attract customers to business class and if business passengers would value the amenities enough to pay a 20-percent premium. Through experimentation with load factors, ABC found the routes on which the expandable business-class section made sense at a 20-percent premium.

The proper ratio between perceived value or usefulness and price can be difficult to achieve. If the perceived value of a product is low, few will pay a high or even moderate price for it. On the other hand, if the price of a high-quality product or service is low, consumers may think the low price indicates low quality and may therefore not avail themselves of the product or service. When Sara Lee offered an excellent cheesecake at a low price, the company expected customers to see it as a great buy. Customers, however, thought that a cheesecake priced that low could not be very good. When the company raised the price, sales boomed. Services provided free by governmental agencies and paid for by third parties can experience similar problems. Counseling and psychotherapy involving third-party payment can be seen as "cheap" by clients, and this perception can interfere with their involvement. Flatow (1986) suggests that pricing should never be the lead element in a marketing strategy. He points out that frozen dinners by Budget Gourmet are not just low priced; they are good main meals at a lower price.

Quantity, too, can affect the value-price ratio. The quantity should be enough to satisfy the customer's need. For instance, some people disparage so-called nouvelle cuisine, not because of the taste, but because the portions are too small to satisfy them. The aesthetics of a beautifully laid out plate of a small fillet of fish and a few al dente vegetables are no substitute for what they see as a reasonable quantity.

RENEWED FOCUS ON QUALITY

Some people buy low-quality products or services because, for them, the value-price ratio is favorable. They put up with annoyances—electric fans that begin to clatter a week after they are purchased, automobiles with knobs that fall off and trunks that have to be slammed shut, laundries that lose shirt buttons, and counseling sessions that go nowhere—either because they have come to expect little from products and services or because their needs and wants are easily satisfied or because they focus exclusively on low prices.

Nevertheless, value is being related more and more to quality. If a consumer is wondering which make of car to buy, he or she may

very well test-drive several cars. If a gear shift requires a lot of tug-
ging and pushing to change gears, the consumer will probably realize
there is a quality problem and decide on another make. The following example, however, is in sharp contrast to the poor-quality
automobile.

> EXAMPLE: I heard a group of 3M managers talking about quality.
> I thought I understood what they were saying, so I commented, "Then
> defective parts or products don't even leave your plants." They stared
> at me grimly, then one replied, "We don't *make* defective parts or
> products."

In industries in which competition has become fierce and worldwide,
there is an intense focus on quality (Crosby, 1980, 1984; Groocock,
1986; Juran, 1985; Townsend, 1986). Consumerism means that more
and more customers are becoming aware of their rights and are refusing to accept poor-quality products and services. The current slogan
of the Ford Motor Company is "Quality is job one." Ford's Taurus
and Sable models hit the bull's-eye because of improved technology
and high quality. In an advertisement in *Fortune* (September 29, 1986)
General Motors declares its stance on quality:

> We are changing the way we measure quality throughout General
> Motors. A world class car or truck will get a *zero*. No problems. Any
> deviations from GM quality standards will raise the score. Zero-based
> quality measurement is one example of GM's commitment to quality
> improvement.

A Chicago hospital announced that patients dissatisfied with
a service would not have to pay for it. The bland white-bread-and-
cold-coffee fare found in so many institutions was no longer to be
the standard. Ancillary services would be brought up to the quality
standards set for the medical services. In the highly competitive airline
industry, also, quality is essential. United Airlines' foray into Pacific
markets sputtered because of poor quality (Yates, 1987), and United
then had to try to catch up to the high standards set by other Pacific-
Basin airlines (Hornung, 1987).

> EXAMPLE: ABC Airways, too, knew that it had to compete on quality.
> It mounted an extensive advertising campaign that stated categorically

that ABC would not be outdone in the quality of its services. Since ABC had once been known for its arrogance rather than its service, it now had to do double time. ABC wanted all employees to take pride in the quality of its services. From the time passengers first contact the reservations agents to the moment they leave the airport after the return trip, they must come into contact with concerned ABC personnel. If these employees are both able and willing to provide quality services, the passengers will be far more willing to travel on ABC again. In addition, a great deal of the quality of work life at ABC must come from working for a winner and also from belonging to a company that puts quality of service first.

It has been suggested that the two pillars of success for a company competing in today's turbulent environments are quality of products and service (a productivity factor) and employee participation (a QWL factor).

Quality-Assurance Framework

Quality is easy to espouse but may be difficult to deliver consistently. Crosby (1980), Groocock (1986), Juran (1985), and Townsend (1986) maintain that sustained quality cannot be delivered without a system-wide quality-promotion plan. The following quality-assurance framework is drawn from these authors:

1. **Managers.** Get managers of relevant units involved. They need to know that assuring quality is an area of managerial, not just technical, responsibility.

2. **Publicity.** Publicize the effort. There should be some kind of announcement about the centrality of quality, such as "We will be doing things differently and it will be better for everyone." Tell workers, tell the world.

3. **Prevention.** Emphasize prevention rather than remedy. Dramatize the cost of quality control as a remedial process in terms of lost customers, rejects, the need for large customer-service staffs, and so forth. Measure the costs of falling short of quality standards.

4. The Chain of Quality. Make it clear that quality is to be everybody's business. Get teams behind efforts to improve quality. Early on, identify weak spots in the chain and take remedial action quickly. One person or unit can destroy the work of all the others.

5. Internal/External Customers. Make it clear that the quality program applies to delivery of products and services to internal customers as well as external customers. Also make sure that all employees know who their internal customers are.

6. Actual and Perceived Quality. Make certain that everyone understands the two facets of quality: (a) quality of fact, that is, the conformity of the product or service to high standards; and (b) quality of perception, that is, the perception on the part of customers that their needs are actually more than satisfied by the product or service.

7. Zero Defects. Do not tolerate defects in products and services. The ideal is zero complaints because products and services are of high quality and customers experience them as such.

8. Rewards. Celebrate and reward success in the delivery of high-quality products and services. Demonstrate from the beginning that poor quality will not be tolerated.

9. Organizational Culture. Make quality part of the overt culture of the company or institution. Make sure that there is a set of beliefs, values, and norms that support a "culture of quality."

The following questions can be used as a check list in assessing the delivery of products or services:

- Is it clear to everyone in the organization that products and services that satisfy customer needs constitute the heart of our business?

- Do our products and services meet our clients' needs and wants? Are they valued by our customers?

- What do our products and services offer that makes them different from and better than those of our competitors?

- Do we deliver high-quality products and services? How do we know?
- Do we have a quality-assurance plan or program?
- Do we deliver our products and services in a timely fashion?
- Do we try to compete on quality rather than price?
- To what degree do we continually try to upgrade our products and services?

EXCELLENCE IN CUSTOMER SERVICE

The value of many otherwise excellent products and services is often destroyed or at least blemished by the way in which customers or clients are handled. Effective customer service is no longer an amenity that can be sacrificed when things get tight. In Zemke's (1986a) words:

Customer service is in. The reason is simple: The American economy is now dominated by industries that perform rather than produce. As a result, service and satisfaction have become broad responsibilities that relate very directly to bottom-line success. And as more and more organizations get the word that efficient, consistent "doing" plus first-class customer treatment equal repeat business, the calls for broad-scale customer-service training get louder. (p. 41)

A more basic reason for excellence in customer service is respect for customers and clients. I wince as I observe the shabby ways in which customers and clients are sometimes treated by so-called human-service organizations—schools, governmental agencies, health-care institutions, and churches. Students are poorly treated by teachers, deans, people in the bursar's office, housing officials, and personnel in the registrar's office. It makes one wonder if university employees have ever heard one word about customer service.

The Service Triangle

Albrecht and Zemke (1985) talk about the "service triangle" (pp. 39-43). Each angle of the triangle constitutes one of the three interacting features that need to be in place if excellent service is to be delivered. These are service strategy, effective front-line people, and customer-friendly systems.

1. Service Strategy. Every company or institution needs a well-conceived strategy for service. The service strategy is a vision, an idea, a guiding concept, a rallying cry, a gospel that permeates the system and helps everyone in it to focus on the real priorities of customers. Even banks, notoriously high-handed in dealing with clients, are waking up. In its mission statement, the First National Bank of Chicago declares that "the customer is First Chicago's highest priority. . . .We will enter into each relationship in the spirit of long-term partnership, aimed at making our customers' interests our interests." Barnett Banks in Florida has adopted a culture of service (Ricks, 1987). The human needs of customers are carefully attended to. Others scoff and say that such a strategy is too expensive; but, so far, Barnett has done very well.

2. Effective Front-Line People. Every company or institution needs customer-oriented front-line people, the kind of people that easily attune themselves to the customer's current situation, need, and frame of mind. Such people will be attentive and responsive. A misguided seminary staffed its telephones with retirees with no phone skills. Many callers received their first impression of the institution from these unskilled people. Frequently the impression was that the seminary was a third-rate institution. Customer-commitment statements—like the one by First Chicago—must be backed up with people who are skilled in customer relations and committed to service.

3. Customer-Friendly Systems. Every company or institution needs customer-friendly systems. The physical facilities, policies, procedures, methods, and communication processes must all say to the customer, "Everything here is designed to serve you." A shoe firm stated in its advertisements that they were so confident in the quality of a new line of shoes that customers could wear them for thirty days and then return them if they were not completely satisfied. However, when customers actually did return the shoes, they had to fill out long forms, they were made to feel guilty, and they were pressured into buying another line. For most of us, a cursory review of our own experiences as customers or clients will suggest that business and institutions with a sense of service are few and far between.

The Horrors of Repairs

Most people have complained at one time or another about how difficult it is to get things repaired. Trachtenberg (1986) points out some of the economic reasons for this. For instance, the rise of discount retailers has led to the elimination of the service and repair desks. On the manufacturing side, automated processes do not lead to products that are easy to repair. Customers are asked to ship defective articles back to the manufacturer, but they are reluctant to do so. Furthermore, since people who repair goods are frequently not highly paid and since repair work is often not seen as a prestigious job, the best people usually end up in other types of work. Trachtenberg also points out another factor:

> The macroeconomics of our era is that the economics of manufacturing are now highly favorable, while the economics of repair are highly unfavorable. If repairs were simpler to complete, surely service costs would go down. But who would exchange today's fast, sophisticated computers for models that performed far less efficiently but were easier to repair? (p. 73)

This may lead us to wonder if there is any hope for repairs or if the current economic environment will win out. In looking at what the exemplars in the field of repairs do, Trachtenberg (1986) describes how General Electric has tackled the problem:[1]

---

[1]Excerpted by permission of *Forbes* magazine, July 14, 1986. © Forbes, Inc., 1986.

General Electric is the only major appliance manufacturer offering such service nation wide. Four years ago GE discovered that its customers were dissatisfied with the repairs its 2,000 technicians were providing. The company issued uniforms to replace the T shirts and jeans its repair people had worn, and blue vans to replace their station wagons. GE also established a 24-hour 800 number to answer repair or service questions for its consumer product line that fields 50,000 calls a week.

Listen to Stephen O'Brien, vice president of sales and service in GE's major appliance division: "We realized our technicians had as many as 3 million contacts a year with consumers. If the job is done right, it creates terrific brand loyalty. And it's easier to do it right when you control the service, not a franchiser."

The company sends out 700,000 customer response cards as a follow-up to visits from its repairmen, and O'Brien says nearly 40% of those cards are returned. Service managers and repairmen are then graded on customer satisfaction, not the number of stops they make each day.

"Those cards are the number one criterion for determining salary," says O'Brien. "We've gone from a rating in the low 80's to the low 90's. We consider those repairman-customer contacts more beneficial to us than national advertising." Good service is a form of marketing for Sears and GE—and a modest profit center, GE insists.

General Electric has established a service *system*, including rewards for meeting the objectives of the system. All companies and institutions, then, need to find, over and over again, improved ways of obeying the excellence injunction touted by Peters and Waterman (1982), "Stay close to your customers."

INTERNAL CUSTOMERS

Everything that has been said about the delivery of quality products and services in the spirit of customer satisfaction to external customers applies to internal customers as well. If people do not deliver quality products and services to the person at the next desk or the next station, then the entire process breaks down. As Robson (1986) says:[2]

---

[2]From *Journey to Excellence* (p. 54) by M. Robson, 1986, Chichester (United Kingdom): John Wiley. Copyright 1986 by John Wiley. Reprinted with permission.

What we have left, then, is the job of. . .persuading people that the internal customer is as important as the external customer, and of training people in the skills required to deal with customers. The training that is needed is exactly the same as that relevant to training in external customer orientation; there is not a syllable of difference in the skills required and so we can, as of now, forget the distinction between internal and external and refer to both simply as customers. (p. 54)

For some organizational units, the very identification of and communication with internal clients will constitute a revolution. The CEO of Scandinavian Airlines (SAS), Jan Carlzon (1987), referred to the fifty thousand "moments of truth" per day experienced by front-line SAS employees in dealing with customers. He said that the SAS organizational pyramid needed to be turned on its side so that it would be clear to everyone that the job of those higher up was to help front-line people deal with customers effectively, making the vast majority of those fifty thousand moments of truth swing in favor of SAS. Internal units must serve one another if front-line people are to satisfy customers.

The following questions may help you assess the quality of customer service in your system:

- Do we have a realistic and viable customer-service strategy?
- To what extent does this strategy include both external and internal customers?
- Do we have customer-oriented front-line people?
- How customer-friendly are our internal systems, that is, our physical facilities, policies, procedures, methods, and communication processes?
- To what degree are customers or clients systematically asked for feedback?
- How effective is the response to this feedback?
- What do our customers think of our dealings with them?
- How easy is it for customers and clients to make their concerns known to the people in the organization who can manage these concerns?

- How responsive is the organization to customer or client needs, wants, and concerns?
- What kind of priority do good customer and client relationships have with us?
- To what degree are fresh approaches to client relationships developed and implemented?

MAINTAINING A STRATEGIC PERSPECTIVE

Strategy, to be effective, needs to be driven down into the heart of the company or institution, influencing operational and organizational decisions. Haas (1987, p. 76) uses the term *strategic breakpoint* and defines it as "a point where an incremental improvement in some value parameter (price, quality, or service) will trigger a disproportionate volume increase and tilt the competitive balance." For instance, during the early years of the competition between American and Japanese automakers, time between repairs for Toyotas and American cars was roughly the same. However, when Toyota was able to increase quality to the point that its average car needed repairs only every six months while the average American car needed attention every seven weeks, then the gap became noticeable and buyers flocked to Japanese cars. This was a strategic breakpoint. Each company or institution can ask itself, "What product-related, service-related, or customer-relation-related strategic breakpoints can be achieved by us?" This question can be answered only if there is a strategic mentality in the organization and if innovative thinking about products, services, and customer relations is part of the organizational culture.

8

Work Programs

DESIGNING PRODUCTIVITY AND QUALITY
OF WORK LIFE INTO THE SYSTEM

Work programs are those step-by-step processes or tasks through which services are designed and delivered or products are manufactured, assembled, marketed, and sold. Since work programs are carried out by people—except in the case of automation—the way the programs are designed has direct QWL (quality-of-work-life) implications. Ideally, work programs are clear, step-by-step, concise, and cost-efficient processes that lead to the delivery of high-quality products or services. From a QWL point of view, work processes should not only not harm the workers who carry them out, but they should also contribute to the workers' growth and development.

In most companies and institutions there are, of course, multiple interrelated work programs. In manufacturing concerns there are step-by-step processes in research and development, manufacturing, marketing, sales, accounting, personnel, purchasing, and building maintenance; in educational settings there are work programs for school administration, teaching, library management, physical education, athletic programs, and social events; in churches, programs for liturgical celebrations, counseling, hospital visitations, publications, and financial management; in hospitals, procedures in admissions, nursing, laundry, laboratories, surgery, intensive care, and the pharmacy. Some work programs are extremely complex, for example, the vast web of programs needed to produce an automobile. The scheduling and coordination of these processes are formidable tasks, as indicated by Galbraith (1977):

> In the late 1950s and early 1960s a good deal of research was devoted to finding a solution to the job-shop scheduling problem. This is a very

complex combinatorial problem. For example, if there are five parts, each requiring work on a sequence of five different machines, then there are 25 billion possible ways to schedule the parts which need to be evaluated prior to choosing the best one. Even this extremely simple example would require computer time amounting to several centuries of 24-hour days to solve it. (p. 81)

Even with the faster computers of the Eighties this task would be formidable. Complex outcomes require complex work programs. This means that the major steps of a program must be divided into substeps, and each of the substeps will also have its own set of work programs. This is the way automobiles are put together on assembly lines; this is the way that animals are trained to perform their amazing feats. Complexity in any system or subsystem demands coordination and attention to detail.

Even managerial activities such as coaching and couseling involve relatively complex work processes, although at first glance they may not seem to do so. One manager, during an interview prior to a course on coaching and counseling skills, looked plaintively at the interviewer and said: "When—as actually happened last week— one of my staff members comes in, begins to talk about how her marriage is falling apart, and collapses in tears, what do I do?" He really wanted to know "What needs to be done and in what sequence?" It is easier to answer that question if one has a clear idea of the range of meaningful *outcomes* in such a situation. "What do I do?" (work program) is actually question No. 2. The No. 1 question is "What would I like to accomplish?" (product, outcome, accomplishment).

The logic is simple. When work programs are well orchestrated and executed, products and services are delivered in each of a system's major categories, and its mission is accomplished because relevant needs and wants of clients or customers are satisfied. But organizations are not always that logical.

The Tyranny of Work Programs in Human Services

In human-service systems, people sometimes say *program* when they mean *system*. For instance, people may say that they want to set up a training program when they mean (at least in the language of Model A) that they want to establish a training-delivery system. The problem is more than semantic. Since work programs denote a range of activities and only indirectly denote the accomplishments toward which these activities are directed, establishing a training program rather than a training system can, as Gilbert (1978) points out, lead to a great deal of activity (work programs) and few accomplishments (valued outcomes).

Establishing a training *system* (as a part of a larger system) means identifying the needs and wants of those being trained, developing mission statements, identifying major categories of training outcomes, developing specific outcomes in each category, and establishing step-by-step work programs for the accomplishment of these outcomes. That is, Model A is a blueprint for designing a training subsystem as part of a larger system. One reason that training programs can be so notoriously cost ineffective (see Gilbert, 1978, for a discussion of this point) is that they are a set of activities rather than systems. This is an example of the "tyranny of programs." When the outcomes of human-service systems are not clearly identified, then Parkinson's (1986, p. 14) law, "Work expands so as to fill the time available for its completion," can rule the day.

The fact that outcomes may not be clear in a service system does not mean that people are not working hard. Many people in the military or human-service professions such as management, counseling, and the ministry claim that they work such long hours that their marriages are in jeopardy or that the quality of family life is suffering. In these cases, probably one of two things is true. First, they may like their work and find it so rewarding that they are willing to put in the extra hours despite some unpleasant side effects. Alternately, they may be victims of the tyranny of programs. If "working hard" is a cultural value in any given system, then the probability is increased that the employees will engage in activities that are not directed toward clearly defined outcomes.

Tsongas (1981), in discussing mistakes made by liberal politicians, presents a different kind of tyranny of programs:

> Many liberals failed to make a distinction between values [as part of mission] and programs. A liberal program devised in pursuit of a given value was held to be sacrosanct, even if it was inappropriate, ineffective, or abused; the program itself became the object of loyalty, not

the value it was intended to serve. Thus, when CETA was used as a source of patronage by many of the nation's mayors and county officials, the value [mission] was not being served. Liberals hurt themselves and ultimately their own values by not being willing to recognize the abuse of CETA and moving rapidly and convincingly to correct it. Instead, CETA was defended pretty much as is, and the electorate rebelled. (p. 243)

This is an excellent example of self-defeating arationality in systems. Politics and self-interest led to a tyranny of programs that probably seemed useful in the short run but certainly proved otherwise in the long run.

PRINCIPLES OF WORK-PROGRAM DEVELOPMENT

The following principles can be used as an outline, guide, or check list for developing work programs.

1. Link Work Programs Clearly to Outcomes.

If outcomes are not clear, then it is impossible to link programs to them. In this case there is the temptation to make the work program clear and hope that it will achieve the right goal instead of returning to the sometimes irritating task of outcome clarification. If you are having trouble establishing work programs, consider the possibility that your outcomes are not clear enough. Linking work programs to outcomes is needed in a special way in human-service systems, as illustrated in the following example.

> EXAMPLE: A group of faculty members led by the director of behavioral medicine at a large medical school wanted to do something about "humanizing" doctors-to-be. They managed to have the faculty senate mandate a course in human relations skills for first-year medical students. At the end of the first year a consultant was called in, because the program had proved to be a flop. The medical students hated it.
> When the consultant examined the work program with the faculty, he discovered that they had based it on what might be called a

"human-potential" model of communication-skills training. The students were asked to reveal personal things about themselves to one another and to practice such skills as effective listening and empathic responding as they did so. In brief, the students hated the course because they thought it had little or nothing to do with medicine. The consultant suggested a medical problem-management model as the basis of the communication-skills training program. This model included examining patients, making diagnoses, determining interventions, delivering medical or surgical interventions, and evaluating the results. Doing all this effectively and humanely would require a range of communication skills. Examinations included tests, hands-on approaches, and listening to the patient. "If you listen carefully to the patient, he or she will tell you what is wrong" is part of traditional medical wisdom.

In practice sessions, students played the role of patients. Once basic communication skills were taught in the context of a medical model and through work programs in keeping with this model, they seemed much more relevant to the students. Their professors found that they could make the same kinds of demands on students for excellence in the area of doctor-patient communication that other faculty members were making in other medical areas.

2. Examine a Variety of Different Ways of Delivering Outcomes.

Do not make the mistake of putting in place the first work program that comes to mind. Keeping an open mind with respect to different paths to outcomes can contribute to both the effectiveness and the efficiency of work programs. Imagination is critical. In a recent article (Merwin, 1986) a Honda plant and a Jeep plant were contrasted:[1]

For one factory [Honda], these are the best of times. . . . For the other factory, it is quite a different story. While the [latter] plant's product [the Jeep], a natural in today's segmented auto market, is selling briskly, its habits and hardware are old. . . . Honda and Jeep have one thing in common: output. Each working day Honda turns out 875 four-wheel passenger vehicles. . . . Jeep produces 750 of the machines. Beyond that,

[1]Adapted by permission of *Forbes* magazine, June 16, 1986, pp. 101-103. © Forbes, Inc., 1986.

the similarities end. Honda produces its vehicles in 1.7 million square feet of tightly organized floor space, while Jeep fills more than three times that amount. Honda needs 2,432 autoworkers to produce its cars. Jeep requires slightly more than twice that number. . . . Some of the difference is attributable to American car manufacturers' habit of offering so many options. . . . Honda stamps out long runs of nearly identical cars, which is a far more efficient method. From where welding begins at Honda's plant until the finished car is fueled and driven off the line, no human moves the car—it is done entirely by hooks or conveyors. At Jeep, by contrast, production lines are broken at several places, requiring carriers and partially assembled car bodies to be dragged manually from one line to the next. . . . The Jeep line snakes up and down through most of the factory's maze of 64 interconnected buildings. . . . The whole Rube Goldberg arrangement prevents Jeep from using a pure "just-in-time" inventory control, as Honda does. A walk through the Honda plant reveals not only automation in place for today but also what's being added weekly for the future. Here's a robot. . . spraying adhesive on a dashboard, a process that only one month ago was done by hand. Nearby stands a machine picking up windshields and laying them in place, a job done by two humans a few days earlier. (pp. 101-103)

To be fair, we must admit that Honda started with a new plant, whereas Jeep lives on with the inefficiencies of the old. However, the same kind of research-and-development mentality that is directed toward improving products and services is needed to create more effective and efficient work processes. Now that Chrysler, which prides itself on cost-effective manufacturing, has taken over Jeep, we can probably expect more streamlined work programs.

New ways of delivering products and services can greatly benefit customers and clients. An article in *Business Week* (September 29, 1986) announces a new method of administering estrogen that promises to reduce the undesirable side effects of the hormone:

Ciba-Geigy Corp. will market a skin patch that slowly releases a small dose of the natural hormone estradiol. The patches, which are already used to provide nitroglycerin to patients with angina and scopolamine to prevent motion sickness, allow the drug to be absorbed through the skin directly into the bloodstream. Since the estrogen won't have to pass through the digestive tract, the required dose is only one-tenth that of the pill form. In addition, the natural hormone, which would be destroyed in the stomach, produces fewer side effects than the synthetic version used in the pills.

The same kind of inventiveness can be used to devise more effective and efficient work programs in human-service systems, too. In fact, education books and journals are filled with new and more effective ways of stimulating learning. The trouble is that few seem to find their way into the classroom.

3. Look for Exemplars.

An exemplar is a person or a system that delivers high-quality products or services on time and at the lowest cost. Exemplars are people or systems that "do it best." Looking for exemplars is another way of searching for the best-fit program instead of settling for the first one that comes along. Whatever the task, the questions that need to be answered are "Who else is doing this? Who is doing it best in terms of quality and cost effectiveness? Who is developing new, better, and more efficient technologies?"

> EXAMPLE: A psychologist working in a VA hospital was putting most of her time into direct service to patients. She was approaching burnout. After returning from a visit to a hospital in which psychologists spent a fair amount of their time training paraprofessionals, she began to spend much more time in training aides and others who had extensive direct contact with patients in communication, patient-care, teamwork, and problem-management skills. She taught them how to run goal-oriented group sessions with patients. From then on she spent much more time developing training programs for both paraprofessionals and patients and supervising the work of paraprofessionals.

In this case, both productivity and quality of life improved because of the new work program. Perhaps one reason that human-service systems, including the service-oriented subunits of organizations and industries, remain inefficient is that they fail to look for innovative technologies that enable human services to be delivered more effectively and efficiently. At any rate, the final work program tends to be better if it is the one that is chosen from among a number of possibilities. Having a number of possibilities also means that contingency programs can be relied on in case the first-choice work program proves to be flawed.

4. Establish Criteria for Adopting Work Programs.

The criteria for choosing programs are effectiveness, efficiency, and quality of work life in the system.

Effectiveness. The questions here are "Will this work program, if implemented, actually achieve the intended outcome?" and "Will it deliver the necessary quality?" Jeep's method of moving cars along the assembly line works (it is effective), but it takes longer and requires more workers (it is relatively inefficient). In order to set up effectiveness criteria, outcomes—whether products (a toaster, an automobile) or services (an airline flight, the delivery of an express package, an operation, or a counseling session)—and the standards by which the outcomes are judged must be clear.

Efficiency. If it is clear that a number of different work programs will be effective, then the next question is "Which program is most efficient in terms of time, money, and effort?" That is, which program makes the best use of the resources of the system? In a competitive environment, even high-quality products or services that are overpriced because of the inefficiencies of work programs may not sell.

EXAMPLE: An instructor who was training recently hired sales people in sales techniques realized that an inductive, experiential approach to training was more costly in terms of time, effort, and money. It also required an assistant and that would add to the cost. She found that she was much more tired at the end of the day when she used experiential approaches rather than lectures. However, her research had indicated that the trainees were more highly motivated, learned and retained the techniques better, and used them more frequently on the job when she used hands-on approaches. She ultimately chose a training program that was partly inductive and partly deductive. It cut down on the cost and was almost as effective as a totally deductive approach.

In building both effectiveness and efficiency into work programs, care must be taken to maintain a *strategic perspective*. The notion of *strategic breakpoints* (Haas, 1987), mentioned in Chapter 7, also applies to work programs:

> A U.S. printed-circuit-board fabricator achieved a strategic breakpoint by adopting an innovative production process that looked uneconomical in operational terms. Wanting to cut costs, management had asked its engineers to experiment with a new chemical deposition process for making printed-circuit boards. When the engineering team had finally worked out all the bugs, management learned that the new technology would add 30% to the boards' cost. But it would also produce denser boards of better quality that could be sold at high margins in a specialty market. An operationally unattractive process turned out to make superb strategic sense. (p. 76)

Note how market, product, and manufacturing process (work program) are all intimately linked to the strategic perspective. Managers of companies and institutions need to ask themselves over and over again, "Does what we are doing operationally and organizationally make *strategic* sense?"

5. Shape the Work Program: Systematically Design Major Steps and Substeps.

Once you have made a decision about which general work program to pursue, move on to mapping out the program in all its practical detail. Unless the product or service and the work program needed to deliver it are quite simple, it is most useful to map out or diagram the entire work program. A diagram or flow chart of what needs to be done to get from Point A to Point B can be relatively simple or quite complicated. The more complicated the work program is, the greater the need for the diagram. Some kind of visual representation of the program will help you see the interrelationships more clearly, arrange the parts more effectively, and understand problem areas more thoroughly.

In arranging steps and substeps, it is useful to play around with the order in which steps are done. The general question is "Which step needs to be done first, which second, and so forth?" A question that deals with time and economy is "Which steps can be done concomitantly?" Poorly designed and executed projects and work programs lead to such problems as cost overruns, failures to deliver outcomes on time, worker inefficiency, poor morale, and personnel turnover. There are a variety of books and workbooks available to help with project and work-program design (e.g., Archibald, 1976; Fusco & Posner, 1982; Martin, 1976; Miller, 1974) and a complete range of practical project-management computer software packages (Zemke, 1984, lists over twenty of them). These programs are useful, not just in industrial settings, but also in service settings such as training departments (Lorey, 1983).

PERT (Program Evaluation and Review Technique) was created by the U.S. Navy to plan and control the activities of hundreds of subcontractors in building the first Polaris missile submarine. PERT is a technique that helps managers plan and control activities (work programs) to make sure that a project is completed or a product or service is delivered on time (Miller, 1974). In PERT-like project-management programs, an "event" is the start or completion of a specific task, a "milestone" is the completion of a major phase of a project, and "activities" are the actual tasks in the project. Although unexpected complications (e.g., a strike or a delayed delivery) can put a project off course, PERT-like programs can help both product and service systems develop the kind of bias toward action that Peters and Waterman (1982) found characteristic of successful enterprises: They carefully plan their work programs to get things done.

Figure 8-1 is a simple example of a PERT profile or chart used in developing a training program on dealing with sexual harassment. Scheduling or rescheduling work programs is much easier when one uses a chart of the interrelated activities that must be completed in order to deliver a product or service. It is easy to imagine how extensive some PERT profiles are and how useful new computer programs are in generating them (Sandberg-Diment, 1986).

6. Build QWL into Work Programs.

If a company or institution has a people mission together with the overall strategy and policies needed to implement it, then it is much more probable that QWL considerations will be designed into work programs and not merely tacked on. Work programs can entail not only monetary but also psychological costs in terms of stress. Highly stressful work environments can lead to both psychological and physical damage. Research suggests that work days lost through stress contribute significantly to labor costs. The literature on work design—or work redesign for work programs already in place (Hackman & Oldham, 1980; Kelly, 1982; Robertson & Smith,

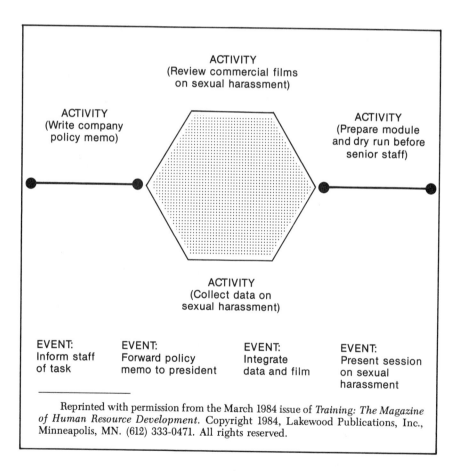

Figure 8-1. A Simple Training Project "P.E.R.T.ed" Out

1985)—suggests a number of ways of designing QWL into work programs. The Hackman and Oldham model is the basis for the framework discussed below.

Hackman and Oldham suggest that three critical psychological states lead to both productivity and QWL: (1) experienced meaningfulness of work, (2) experienced responsibility for the outcomes of work, and (3) knowledge of the actual results of work activities. In determining how work programs can be designed to produce those states, we will consider each state separately.

Experienced Meaningfulness of Work. Three things help people experience work as meaningful. First, *skill variety*. This means that the job requires the worker to perform different activities that call for different skills. Job rotation is one way to increase the variety of skills used. Second, *task identity*. This means that workers are responsible for a meaningful portion of the work. They do a "whole" something rather than a part so small that it seems insignificant. A team of workers in an automobile plant might be responsible for finishing the entire inside of the car. Third, *task significance*. This means that the job is seen to have an impact on others or contributes to the overall mission of the organization. For instance, the people in the planning department see their work incorporated into the strategic and operational plans of the system.

Experienced Responsibility for the Outcomes of Work. The main thing that helps people experience responsibility for the outcomes of work is *autonomy*. Work programs deal with how to deliver outcomes. As far as possible, the how-to details should be left to those responsible for carrying out the program. Activities are often performed more effectively and efficiently if the worker participates in determining them. In highly bureaucratic systems job descriptions are usually very detailed and even minor steps in programs are spelled out in detail. Although this method ensures a great deal of control and predictability in the system, it can eliminate creativity. In many cases, freedom to exercise creativity in the execution of work programs coupled with accountability would contribute more to both productivity and QWL. If people can deliver an outcome effectively and efficiently by doing it their own way with the guidance of predetermined criteria, than there is little reason to insist that it be done the "company" way.

Knowledge of the Actual Results of Work Activities. Workers usually find it rewarding to know they are on course toward objectives. Finding out they are off course can also be rewarding, because it enables them to make the corrections needed to do a good job. Therefore, work needs to be so designed that workers receive feedback from the work itself. Feedback from others (peers or supervisors) can certainly complement this process but cannot take its place. Educational systems in which students do not know how they are doing—or even whether or not they are learning—until they take an examination violate this principle and corrupt the learning process. The number of schools that violate this principle seems to be legion.

> EXAMPLE: "How are you doing in geometry?"
> "I don't know. I haven't had the exam yet."

Hackman and Oldham (1980, p. 82) do not see this model as providing an immediate fix for what ails companies and institutions: "Some employees 'take off' on jobs that are high in motivating potential; others are more likely to 'turn off.'" The Hackman and Oldham model, although useful, is only part of the QWL picture.

Kelly (1982) criticizes the model for things such as being overly psychological, ignoring the power of economic factors (many people work harder for higher wages), and underestimating the impact of the organizational environment. Kelly broadens the picture by exploring four ideologies that can underlie job redesign. First, job redesign can be used by *unitarists*, that is, managerial technicians who are wedded to the status quo and interested only in productivity. Second, *pragmatic pluralists*, such as Hackman and Oldham, use job redesign to foster both increased productivity and improved QWL. Third, *committed pluralists*, concerned mainly with the workers' economic interests, push for worker involvement in job redesign projects. They see companies and institutions as political entities. Fourth, there are the *radicals*, socialist in their focus, who see organizations in relation to the entire society. They tend to criticize job redesign more than they support it.

Job redesign is presented here as one possible way of increasing QWL. As suggested earlier, QWL considerations need to be designed into the system from the very beginning. A company or institution that is adrift because it has an inadequate mission or strategy provides workers with QWL hazards just as does one with poorly designed work programs.

The following questions will help assess work programs and QWL considerations:

- How clear are the desired accomplishments (products or service outcomes) toward which the work program is directed? How well do we know what we are doing?

- To what degree is there a clear, step-by-step work program for every outcome?

- Have we made sure that each work program is as simple and as cost effective as possible? If so, how?

- In the case of complex work programs, how clearly and effectively are subprograms integrated with one another?

- To what degree has the efficiency of complex work programs been determined by some systematic programing methodology, such as PERT?

- To what degree have QWL considerations been designed into the work programs?

- How well do the work programs provide variety, a sense of completeness, and meaning?

- To what degree can workers give themselves ongoing feedback on their performance?

- How well do we build a strategic perspective into work-program decisions?

9

Managing Material Resources

Companies and institutions use a variety of material resources in delivering products and services. These include (a) financial resources and (b) other material resources, such as machinery, computers, buildings, tools, rooms, uniforms, furniture, vehicles, and books. System members use these resources to carry out work programs. The task of managing material resources is often a formidable one.

MANAGING FINANCES

In most companies, institutions, and agencies, economics enters every decision-making process. Many businesses fail because they fail to manage money well. Consider the case of CityFed Financial (see Jereski, 1987):

EXAMPLE: CityFed Financial of Palm Beach took an $84 million pretax write-off in January, 1987, which stunned investors. What had happened? When interest rates peaked in 1981, it sharply increased lending activity in that year. The strategy that was pursued agressively was this: Write as many mortgages as possible, sell them to Fannie Mae, then sit back and enjoy the income from servicing the loan. However, CityFed went overboard in its use of accrual accounting. It claimed as immediate profit what it would earn from serving the loan portfolio. This is all right if two projections are correct: (1) the costs of servicing the portfolio and (2) the projected average life of the mortgages. In CityFed's case, neither projection was accurate. It assumed that it could service the portfolio for one-eighth of 1 percent of the amount of the loan instead of the usual one-quarter of 1 percent. For accounting purposes, it kept assuming that the average life of mortgages in its service portfolio would be ten years, when in reality people were refinancing 1984 and 1985 loans within a couple of years.

Faulty accounting procedures lay at the root of the crisis. As Jereski (1987, p. 54) notes, "In the case of mortgage banking. . .better to have the cash in hand before you start bragging about profits."

To remain financially and economically innocent is to court both manipulation and fiscal disaster. Many people in a wide range of companies, institutions, and agencies, even though they are not directly involved with finance, could well become more informed about economic concepts such as financing, pricing, costs, cost accounting, cost control, debt, debt service, equity, overhead, cash flow, profit and loss, taxes, inflation, and the economic environment and outlook. Financial planning should go hand in hand with strategic planning. To be sound, strategic plans must be financially sound. As Fix (1986) points out, Wheeler Airlines blundered in this regard:

"I misread deregulation," Wheeler admits. "I thought it meant we should run off and expand like crazy." Wheeler tripled his fleet, quadrupled the number of airports that he served and wound up with no clear idea of how to manage such an operation—the classic small businessman's mistake of pushing sales growth at the expense of financial controls and profitability.

"At the height of our foolishness we had six single-engine planes, five Beechcraft 99s, a 40% load factor, 55 employees, $5 million in sales and zero profitability," Wheeler recounts. "Our bookkeeper was running 45 days behind. When we finally got smart, we'd lost $800,000 in eight months." (p. 58)

It was no surprise, then, to learn that in late 1985 Wheeler Airlines went into Chapter 11 bankruptcy.

The QWL implications of a business or institution that is in financial trouble are obvious. Recently a college in the midwest went out of business because it could no longer meet its financial obligations. The turmoil among both staff and students during the last months of alternating hope and despair disrupted not just the educational process but the very lives of student, faculty, and staff. The loss of morale in financially troubled systems simply speeds up the process of dissolution.

Money is a critical resource, and finance-related programs are an important but sometimes dimly understood part of the work needed to keep the system alive. It would be healthier if more members of a company or institution were aware of financial realities than just financial officers. There are courses and books on topics such as "finance for the nonfinancial manager" and "managerial accounting and control techniques for the nonaccountant" (e.g., Finkler, 1983; Fleming, 1984; Spiro, 1977).

MANAGING OTHER MATERIAL RESOURCES

The focus here is on choosing and using tools, including computers, new technologies, maintenance programs, and logistics.

Getting the Right Tools and Using Them Well

Productivity is often related to the choice and use of tools. For instance, books are important tools in educational settings. Gilbert (1978) suggests that teachers are hampered because of the textbooks that are currently available. Texts, he says, generally satisfy the interests of authors and publishers rather than teachers and students; that is, they are poor tools. Consider the following anecdote:

> EXAMPLE: The advanced-algebra teacher of my younger brother died suddenly, and another teacher was called in to substitute. One day the substitute asked the students to read a certain chapter of the text. He waited until all the students had finished reading it, then he asked, "How many of you understand what's in that chapter?" No one raised a hand. The teacher said, I read it three times the other night and I still don't understand it. Rip it out." My brother was then sent around the room with the wastebasket to collect the offending chapter.

Perhaps more often than we care to believe, people are accused of incompetence when the real problem is that they are saddled with ineffective materials and tools or have not been trained to use them effectively. It is demoralizing to be asked to produce quality work with poor or inadequate tools. A management development unit in a large institution had to work for three years without the benefit of a desktop computer, not because the system did not have the financial resources to purchase them, but because of the political infighting that went on over larger information-management issues. Both productivity and quality of work life in the unit suffered.

Audiovisual Equipment. It is critical to link material resources to outcomes, that is, the products or services to be delivered. A vast amount of unused audio and video equipment lies in thousands of storage rooms in schools throughout the country. Before ordering such equipment, potential users need to ask, "How will the equipment help us produce better educational outcomes? How easy is it to use? What is the likelihood of its being used by *our* staff? Will people be trained to use it? Is it worth the cost?"

Computers. It is not easy anymore to think of the world of business and industry without computers. When used well, they do marvelous things. However, they need to be integrated into the entire system and not used as a substitute for clear thinking on the part of managers. In discussing how many companies have tried to solve their data-processing problems simply by bringing in computers, Hayes and Clark (1986) describe the situation this way:

> They soon learned that computerizing a poorly organized and error-ridden information system simply creates more problems: garbage in, garbage out. That lesson, learned so long ago, has been largely forgotten by today's managers, who are trying to improve manufacturing performance by bringing in sophisticated new equipment without first reducing the complexity and confusion of their operations. Spending big money on hardware fixes will not help if managers have not taken the time to simplify and clarify their factories' operations, eliminate sources of error and confusion, and boost the rate of learning. (p. 71)

Systems that use computers effectively have clear productivity-related outcomes in mind. In 1979 the Los Angeles County Public Administrator's office faced severe budget cuts that led to a 10-percent decrease in the staff. The decision was made to automate all the department's functions. The following account is from the Los Angeles County Public Administrator (1986):

> The custom-designed trust accounting and management information system . . . is made up of six master modules: General, Estate,

Fiscal Accounting, Property, Conservatorship, and Office Automation.... First-line supervisors and middle management project teams provided input to top management and the contractor for developing written procedures and data output formats. In addition to providing multiple accounting and production monitoring functions, the system includes a case management function that allows the tracking of cases from start to finish.... The system's productivity gains are many.... A total of 450 screens and reports have reduced input documents from 1,002,360 to 83,530 annually. Other productivity gains are achieved by using the system to produce ad hoc reports, legal documents, and electronic worksheets. (p. 30)

In this case the installation of the computer led to a complete realignment of the human resources of the department. Staff members were relocated and trained to use the system. There was a renewed enthusiasm for work. And so a material resource contributed significantly to improve the quality of life of the members of the system. In a word, the members of the department *learned* to work smarter, and this proved to be challenging and exciting. Hayes and Clark's research has convinced them that a system's *learning rate*, that is, the rate at which managers and workers learn to make it run better, is more important than the material resources it uses.

Managing Technology

New technology can be so fascinating in itself that companies and institutions buy and use it without question. They fail to ask such bottom-line questions as "Will this technology help us produce valued products and deliver valued services in cost-efficient ways? How well does this technology fit with QWL considerations? Can we be more efficient by working smarter without the help of costly new technology?" On the other hand, the excellent companies are constantly in search for technologies that deliver higher productivity without impairing QWL. Bylinsky (1986) describes an achievement by Allen-Bradley, which specializes in industrial controls:

The 600 units produced each hour on the automated assembly line are contactors and relays that serve as electromechanical starters and controllers for industrial electric motors. With this futuristic assembly line... Allen-Bradley achieved a milestone in the development of computer-integrated manufacturing, CIM for short: the ability to make different versions of a product at mass-production speeds in lots as small as a single unit...No one else has achieved what John C. Rothwell, manager of the Allen-Bradley line, calls "the dream of the Japanese"—which is "to make goods flow like water through the line." (p. 65)

Although contactors and relays are not as complex as automobiles, Allen-Bradley's remarkable assembly line is a forerunner of the rapid production of more complicated products in lots of one—what Davis (1987) calls "mass customizing." In Chapter 8 we saw that one of the reasons (but hardly the principal reason) that Honda produces cars more efficiently than Jeep does is its strategy of producing cars with relatively few options. With an Allen-Bradley type of break-through, cars with multiple options would be no more difficult to produce. In an analogous way, creativity in the use of simple tools can serve human-service practitioners well. For instance, counselors can become more productive by using simple tools, such as flip charts that clients can use in the counseling sessions for writing out key learn-ings or proposed action steps, pamphlets that enable clients to under-stand their particular problems better, check lists and guides for implementing action plans, videos in which clients can see themselves in action, and audio recorders for reviewing sessions or recording ideas (as they are generated) for the next counseling session. The purpose of these tools is not to fill the counseling process with gimmicks, but to ensure clear understanding of problem situations and facilitate problem-management action on the part of clients.

Maintenance of Material Resources

Material resources need to be kept in good repair for at least two reasons: cost effectiveness and morale. When an essential machine breaks down, it is costly and annoying. Some companies schedule machine maintenance at regular intervals and replace worn parts, because it is difficult to predict when the equipment actually needs servicing. In discussing this difficulty, Port (1986) describes a creative approach:

Palomar Technology International, Inc., hopes to simplify all that. It has developed a portable monitor that makes diagnosing the condition of industrial equipment a breeze. Past data such as operating temperature and vibration are stored in a desktop computer. When it's time for inspection, an engineer slings the 5-lb. portable unit over a shoulder and collects current vibration data with a magnetic probe. He also keys in temperature and pressure readings from gauges on the equipment being tested. Back in the office, the host computer analyzes the data for unusual changes and prints out any trouble signals. (p. 90).

Here a creative technology is used to keep material resources in top shape. Companies and institutions need to weigh the cost of preventive maintenance against the cost of failure to keep material resources in top working order.

The other issue is morale. Poorly maintained facilities send signals that say, "Sloppiness is permitted here," "This company is not doing very well and cannot afford to maintain its physical resources," or "We expect workers to work harder to make up for poorly maintained equipment." Well-maintained physical resources send opposite messages. The very aesthetics of the work place, too, send messages both to workers and to clients.

Logistics

Logistics, according to Webster's dictionary, relates to the procurement, maintenance, and transportation of materiel, facilities, and personnel. Logistics, as used in this chapter, is the art of making sure that material resources are available as they are needed. When working for a company that provided screws, nuts, and bolts to the automotive and home-appliance industries, I learned quickly that it is dangerous to fail to ship material on time. That company's failure to ship an order on time led to the shutdown of an assembly line of a large appliance maker. The company was notified immediately that it would no longer provide the part in question. Furthermore, it was informed that any future failures to meet a schedule would result in its termination as a supplier for the appliance company.

As a sign of the growing importance of logistics, some universities now offer both undergraduate and graduate degrees in this art or science. This is an area in which Japanese companies have done some pioneering, as Galante (1986) explains:[1]

> *Kanban* literally means "card" or "sign." But it has come to denote a parts-supply system devised by Toyota Corporation to keep inventory—and hence inventory carrying costs—to a minimum. Japanese suppliers ship car parts to Toyota in containers, each of which has a card—or kanban—slipped into a side pocket. When a production worker dips into the container for the first time, he sends the card back to the supplier. The supplier places the card into a second container of parts, which, at least in theory, reaches the production worker just as he is attaching the last part from the first box onto a car on the assembly line. This "just-in-time" inventory system works in Japan partly because suppliers are usually clustered around their customers. . . . But in the U.S., where the kanban system has fired the imagination of many cost conscious managers, distances are often much greater. So, U.S. manufacturers are recruiting distribution companies to help implement just-in-time delivery. . . A few years ago, Walgreen Laboratories realized the cost of carrying and managing inventory accounted for about 25% of its total inventory costs. So it decided to reduce its inventory levels, then running about $25 million, by a third. It gave suppliers a Hobson's choice: They could participate in a modified "just-in-time" delivery program, or they were out. . . . Distributors with foresight are already taking kanban to its next logical step. They are turning to their own suppliers and insisting deliveries arrive closer to the time when the distributors have to move the goods out the door. (p. 25)

Kanban is only part of the larger supplier picture. Many manufacturers are no longer choosing suppliers just on the basis of cost. They are choosing suppliers carefully and establishing solid working relationships with them. They contract for both quality and other factors such as just-in-time delivery. The result is a win-win partnership.

    The following questions can be used in the search for excellence in the management of material resources.

---

[1]Reprinted by permission of *The Wall Street Journal.* © Dow Jones & Company, Inc. 1986. All Rights Reserved.

The Management of Financial Resources

- How well are our finances managed?
- To what degree are realistic budgets established and followed?
- How is our budget flexibility related to the changing business needs?
- What kinds of financial problems do we face?
- How effectively are these problems being managed?

The Management of Material Resources

- Do we have access to the material resources we need to get our work done?
- How are we assuring that material resources will be available as needed?
- How well are logistics problems handled?
- Do we have the tools we need to get our work done efficiently and effectively?
- What are our relationships with our suppliers like?
- Are cost-effective programs, such as just-in-time delivery, in place?
- In what kind of repair is our equipment?
- Are preventive maintenance programs in place?
- Is new technology (for manufacturing products or delivering services) periodically reviewed?
- Is cost-effective new techology adopted to make the delivery of programs more effective and efficient?

10

Unit Performance Planning

Whereas *strategic planning* is based on the interaction between markets, customers, the environment, the mission of the system, business values, and the major categories of products and services, the *business plan* is a link between strategy and operations. It deals with the allocation of resources to various units or functions within the company or institution in light of the overall strategy. For instance, if the strategy calls for new managerial and technical skills, then more resources will be allocated to the training function. *Operational planning*, on the other hand, deals with pulling all the resources of the company or institution together to design and deliver services or to design, manufacture, and deliver products. The operational plan pulls together all the interconnected processes and work programs needed to keep the system running and delivering its products and services to customers. In larger companies and institutions, this can be an extremely complex process. Each unit needs to formulate its own yearly operational plan and integrate it—in terms of inputs it requires and the outputs it delivers—with the operational plans of other units.

As important as operational plans are, the focus in this section will be on the *unit performance plan*. The data base for this plan includes the strategic plan of the company or institution, its business plan, the operational plan of the unit, and the relationship of the unit to other units for which it is either supplier or customer.

The purpose of the performance plan is to set operational and organizational priorities for the unit in light of the strategic plan.

If, for instance, ABC Airways intends to expand its service into the Pacific, a top priority for cabin-crew services is to recruit, hire, and train the flight attendants needed for the expansion. Strategic planning covers the longer term. Unit performance planning usually covers one year at a time and focuses on the implementation of strategy. Its purpose can be outlined as follows:

- To integrate unit operations with company strategy.
- To set strategic operational priorities for the unit on an annual basis.
- To help managers allocate resources on an annual basis more effectively.
- To provide the basis for agreed-on performance objectives between workers and managers. That is, the unit performance plan provides the basis for individual performance planning (which will be discussed later).

DEVELOPING A UNIT PERFORMANCE PLAN

The development of unit performance plans is the responsibility of each unit manager in consultation with his or her staff. The plan, once developed, can be used by all individuals working in the unit as a basis for their own individual performance plans. The five elements of the plan are: (1) linkage, (2) performance areas, (3) key performance areas, (4) priority performance objectives, and (5) performance indicators. The corporate training unit of ABC Airways will serve as an example.

1. Establish Strategic Linkages.

Performance planning is a cascading process. It is essential for each unit to link its performance plan to the mission and strategic objectives of the next higher unit and ultimately to the mission and strategic objectives of the company or institution. In ABC, the plans of the corporate training unit need to be linked to the mission, the strategic plans, and the operational plans of the human resources department, which in turn must link its mission and plans to those of ABC Airways itself. The mission and plans of the human resources department, together with the mission, work programs, and budget of the corporate training unit, become the data base for the elaboration of the training unit's performance plan.

2. List All Performance Areas.

All the performance areas should be listed. ABC's training unit must have an updated list of all the tasks and outcomes for which the unit is responsible. Model A, since it can be applied to both the entire corporation and to the subunits within it, provides a comprehensive framework for updating the list. For instance, the *business* performance areas for which the training unit is responsible each year include the following:

- Revising its mission to stay in line with the changing mission of ABC and of the mission of the human resources department.
- Establishing a unit strategic plan based on the overall strategy of both the human resources department and ABC.
- Staying in touch with the training trends within the airline industry.
- Assessing the needs of its internal clients in order to revise the major categories of its training services.
- Developing specific training programs, such as customer-service skills, to meet the needs of its internal clients.
- Developing new work programs to deliver these products.
- Acquiring the material resources, including budgetary resources, needed to deliver its programs.

The *organizational* performance areas for which the training unit is responsible each year include the following:

- Redesigning jobs and designing new jobs to deliver training programs.
- Selecting, deselecting, and redeploying the staff of the training unit in order to deliver training programs as effectively as possible.
- Assessing the development and training needs of the members of the training unit itself and designing training programs for them.

- Restructuring teams for the delivery of new training programs.
- Reviewing and redesigning communication processes within the team.
- Reviewing the leadership needs of the unit.

These tasks are based on the business and organizational elements of Model A.

3. Identify Key Performance Areas.

Key performance areas are those that deserve priority attention during the coming year if the unit is to contribute in significant ways to the overall strategy of the company. Answers to the following questions will help determine which are the key performance areas:

- What areas are in decline and need special attention?
- What areas, if further developed, will help us do our work more effectively and efficiently?
- What areas need special attention because of the changing priorities of the company?

Usually no more than four or five areas will be designated as "key." If too many areas carry this designation, the word loses its significance. ABC's corporate training unit, using the above questions, chooses the following as key performance areas:

In the *business* area of the unit:

a. Reformulating its mission in light of the new ABC mission.

b. Doing a needs assessment of middle managers for the management-development program based on the new ABC strategic plan.

c. Having a management-development program for middle managers designed and ready to go by the end of the year.

In the *organizational* area of the unit:

d. Sending members of the training team to state-of-the-art management-development programs so that they can prepare themselves to deliver in-house programs in this area.

e. Installing and implementing the new corporate performance planning and appraisal system in the training unit itself.

Obviously, the training unit will not drop its other work. Rather, it will give special attention to these five areas.

4. Set Priority Unit Objectives in Each Key Performance Area.

When key performance areas have been selected, two or three major performance objectives should be set in each area. These are the actual outcomes, the critical things that will be accomplished in each key area in order to contribute in significant ways to unit and company strategy. For instance, with respect to the area labeled "d" in the above list, the following objectives are set:

- The best management-development programs in the country will be located.
- Key team members will attend these programs.
- Key learnings from each of these programs will be collated to serve as the basis for the in-house ABC management-development programs.

If these three objectives, together with objectives in the other four key performance areas, are implemented within six months, ABC will be well on its way to establishing a high-quality management-development program for its middle managers.

5. Develop Performance Indicators.

Performance indicators are ways of determining whether an objective has been wholly or partially accomplished. Performance indicators must be clear enough to enable managers, supervisors, and staff members to reach a conclusion independently about full or partial fulfillment of each objective. *Interim* indicators are used throughout the year for ongoing feedback, and *final* indicators are used for year-end review. Some objectives are so simple or clear that indicators are not needed. For instance, the previously mentioned area "d" does not need extensive indicators. Some possible interim indicators for that area are the following:

- A list of best-managed companies in the country will be drawn up.
- A list of the most highly rated, university-based, management-development programs will be drawn up.
- The catalogs for these programs will be obtained and studied.
- The directors of management development at the best-managed companies will be interviewed by phone.
- The directors of highly rated university programs will be interviewed by phone.
- In light of these interviews, visits to some top-rated companies and university programs will be made.

All the items indicate that reasonable efforts are underway to identify the best management-development programs in the country.

Figure 10-1 diagrams the five steps of unit performance planning. As we shall see later, the unit performance plan becomes the basis for the individual plans of each of the members of the corporate training unit. The present chapter deals with the performance-planning part of a total performance-planning-feedback-appraisal system. Whatever this system is called, PPA or MBO (management by objectives), it can constitute a mere bureaucratic make-work set of procedures for managers and staff or it can be a humane, effective instrument for achieving and maintaining business, organizational, and leadership excellence. Routine, overly detailed, and rigid PPA systems are a curse.

The following questions can help in assessing the status of the current unit performance plan:

- To what degree does each unit in our organization have a realistic performance plan?
- How well does this plan translate the overall strategic plan of the company or institution into operational realities?
- How well does this plan integrate the unit with other units for which it is either an internal supplier or customer?
- To what degree does the unit performance plan actually help integrate work programs and drive behavior in the unit?

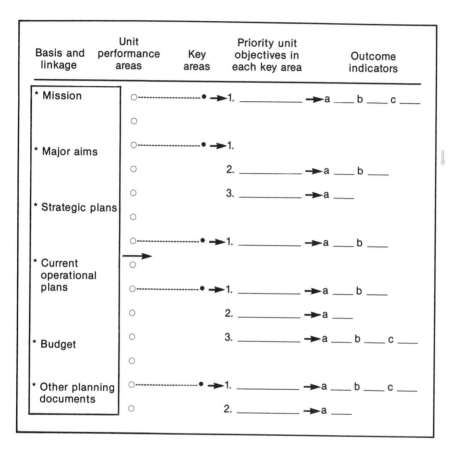

Figure 10-1. The Elements of Unit Performance Planning

- To what degree do the people who work in this unit understand the unit's current strategic priorities?
- Are the objectives of the unit performance plan clear enough to help individuals to establish realistic individual performance plans?
- If there is no unit performance plan, how are unit priorities set?

Figure 10-2 outlines in graphic form some of the main operational considerations in delivering products and services to customers. Again, as in the area of strategy, each enterprise and each unit within the enterprise must come up with its own formula for operational excellence.

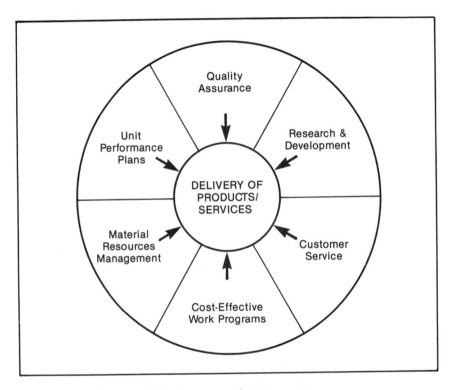

Figure 10-2. Operational Business Dimensions

PART II

ORGANIZATIONAL DIMENSIONS

The Division of Labor

Competent Units with Competent People

Teamwork

Communication Processes

The Reward System

Individual Performance Plans

The organizational dimensions considered in Part II of Model A include structure (the division of labor), competence, teamwork, communication, the reward system, and individual performance planning.

STRUCTURE: THE DIVISION OF LABOR

Some people use the terms *design* and *structure* interchangeably. I prefer to use the term *design* to relate to totality of tasks of Model A, that is, both business and organizational. *Structure*, on the other hand, is an organizational term. It refers to the ways in which a company organizes itself and its processes in order to deliver its products and services. Organizational structure deals with the division of labor and has a double focus: (1) the establishment of different organizational units and (2) the establishment of roles and responsibilities within each of these units. Structure must serve business outcomes.

Organizational Units

Subunits—such as marketing, manufacturing, and human resources—are created to divide up the work of the system. These subunits, too, may be further divided. For instance, the human resources department might include compensation, personnel management, consultancy, and training units. Each unit has its own mission, products or services, and set of work programs that contribute directly or indirectly to the delivery of products and services to external clients or customers. Ideally, only those units are established which are needed to assure the effective delivery of business outcomes. The mission of each unit must be linked to and integrated with the overall mission of the company or institution and to the missions of other units to which it is related as supplier or customer.

Roles and Responsibilities
Within Units

Within each unit roles and responsibilities need to be established. For instance, an accountant in the financial unit needs a defined role and must understand the responsibilities included in that role. Ideally, only necessary roles are established and each person within each organizational unit has a clear idea of what is expected of him or her. On the other hand, there is enough role flexibility to allow for creativity and the management of the unexpected.

Ideally, work is divided up among units and individuals in order to maximize both productivity, that is, effective and efficient business outcomes, and quality of work life.

COMPETENCE

First, if work programs are to be carried out effectively, it is not only necessary to have the right units or functions (the division of labor), but these units need to do *the right things* and do them efficiently. Second, if work programs are to be carried out effectively, it is not only necessary to establish the right roles together with their range of responsibilities, but competent and compatible people need to be hired into these roles.

TEAMWORK

Teamwork refers to the kind of collaboration needed to carry out work programs effectively and efficiently. There are two levels of teamwork. First, organizational units need to collaborate, especially units that relate to one another as internal suppliers or customers. Second, groups and individuals within units need to collaborate in delivering products and services in the pursuit of unit performance objectives. While a spirit of teamwork should characterize the entire company or institution and each of the subunits within it, this does not mean that *every* task needs to be carried out by a team. Both units and individuals within units should work together in teams whenever working together will deliver better business outcomes.

COMMUNICATION

Communication is the lifeblood of the system. Without effective communication the organization limps along or grinds to a halt and teamwork is impossible. For both units and individuals to work well together, they need to share essential information, engage in innovation-promoting and problem-solving dialog, provide confirmatory and corrective feedback, collaborate in appraisal processes, and negotiate conflicts and differences.

THE REWARD SYSTEM

If everything that has been discussed so far in terms of both business and organizational processes is to be carried out, people need reasonable incentives and rewards to do so. Disincentives and unintended punishments need to be identified and controlled. Above all, performance (the effective and efficient delivery of quality products and services to internal and external customers)—rather than nonperformance—must be rewarded.

INDIVIDUAL PERFORMANCE PLANNING

Finally, individual performance planning links the individual within the organization to strategic operational priorities. This is possible, of course, only if the company or institution has a viable strategy, links it to operations through some kind of unit performance plan, and has managers and supervisors that take the time to set priorities with the individuals working within their units.

THE IDEAL

The ideal in all of this is that structure serve function. The units, roles, relationships, communication processes, incentives, and rewards should help to get the work done and the needs of clients met. It goes without saying that structure often serves covert cultural and political purposes rather than productivity and quality-of-life needs.

If all of this is to take place, then effective managerial and supervisory leadership are required. Leadership, then, will be the focus of Part III of Model A.

11

The Division of Labor

In this chapter and the two that follow (one on competence and one on teamwork), first the organizational units will be discussed and then the individuals within the units. If the unit itself is not designed right, then good work on the part of individuals can go for naught.

STRUCTURE: ESTABLISHING SUBUNITS

Subunits, such as marketing, manufacturing, finance, and human resources, are created to divide up the work of the system. These subunits, too, may be further divided. For instance, the human resources department of ABC Airways includes compensation, human resource management, and training units. In hospitals there are a whole range of subunits, including admissions, nursing, the surgical department, the pharmacy, the radiology unit, ambulatory care, the laundry, information-management services, and so forth.

Although entire books are devoted to organizational structure (e.g., Galbraith, 1977) in all its complexities, certain general principles governing the division of labor can be noted here.

• **The Ideal.** Even though there is evidence that certain kinds of organizational structure work better in certain industries (Galbraith, 1977), still there is no one ideal structure for any organization. The one that the organization *makes* work is the best one for it. One of ABC's competitors changed its structure four times in seven years. The problem was not the structure at all, but mismanagement at the top. Changing structure was a smokescreen, a way of pointing a blaming finger at the troops, when it should have been pointed at top management.

- **Purpose.** The purpose of establishing organizational units is to serve business outcomes. Since any given unit tends to see the world from its own perspective, it can along the way begin to serve its own ends and the ends of those who manage it. This is a natural tendency and does not necessarily imply malice on the part of people in the unit. Over time, all organizational units need realignment.

- **Simplicity.** Only those units should be established that are needed to deliver business outcomes or deliver needed assistance to those who are delivering business outcomes. Currently, many organizations are "downsizing," that is, getting rid of unneeded functions and combining the functions that remain. This includes eliminating managerial layers.

EXAMPLE: When strategic planning became an organizational fad, ABC Airways established a strategic planning unit in the personnel department. Many people in the company did not even know that the unit existed, those who knew about it were unclear of its purpose, and no one was sure whether anyone read the stream of reports it produced. In a reorganization endeavor, the unit was eliminated and strategic planning was allocated to the top executive team with input from line managers. The product was a five-year plan that was rolled over and updated yearly (the 1989-1994 plan, the 1990-1995 plan, and so forth), a plan that actually provided the business direction for the company.

In times of growth and prosperity, subunits tend to multiply, especially if competition is mild. Turbulent environments, on the other hand, call for "lean and mean" organizations capable of moving quickly.

- **Reintegration.** Tasks that are assigned to different units need to be reintegrated. This is not always easy. It often happens that certain units develop chronic conflicts with one another, for instance, between manufacturing and sales. Manufacturing does not want to contribute to a costly inventory problem, while the salesperson wants immediate delivery to satisfy customers. An example from my own experience: I ordered some office furniture. There was a long lead time for delivery, and even then the furniture was not delivered on the date promised. After I had signed the contract, I read ads in which an office-furniture manufacturer promised delivery within ten working days. I could only imagine that the latter had worked out the integration of manufacturing and sales more effectively than the manufacturer I had chosen.

The following are questions that can help in assessing the ways in which work has been divided among the units of the company or institution:

- Do we have our structure right? That is, does it enable us to deliver business outcomes efficiently and effectively?
- Which work units in our organization are not really pulling their weight? How much fat is there in the system?
- Could we eliminate or combine any units and still operate quite well?
- How often do we examine and revise our structure to keep up with changes in our business?
- What kind of structure do successful companies or institutions in our business have?
- When we have changed our structure, have the changes led to better business outcomes?
- To what degree have we fallen into the trap of reorganizing when the real problem was that we did not have our business right?

ROLES: GETTING PEOPLE
TO DO THE RIGHT THINGS

In Chapter 8, the whole range of work programs needed to deliver products or services to both internal and external customers was discussed. In this chapter, the roles of the people who execute these work programs are discussed. It may be a question of an executive working on the strategic plan or negotiating a merger or of a nurse giving a patient an injection or assisting in surgery. Each person within the company or institution has a set of responsibilities for delivering products or services to internal or external customers.

Roles can be seen from at least four perspectives:

1. **As a set of responsibilities.** ("John has the responsibility for tracking significant movements on the part of our competitors.")

2. **As a set of tasks to be performed.** ("Eric types, files, and runs errands.")

3. **As a set of expectations that a person has of himself or herself and/or that the organization, supervisors, and colleagues have of that person.** ("Accountant executives are expected to bring in at least three new accounts per month.")

4. **As a set of performance outcomes or accomplishments.** ("If you carry out your supervisory role well, each of your staff members will always have a clear idea of what he or she is doing well and what needs to be improved.")

A person may have more than one role, each with its own responsibilities, tasks, expectations, and outcomes. For instance, faculty members of a counseling psychology program at a university may be expected to teach, do research, counsel in the center for student development, and serve on both departmental and university committees.

Role Clarity

A clear statement of just what roles a person is to play and what tasks he or she is to perform in an organizational unit is called a *job description.* Kellog and Burstiner (1979) suggest that the following elements should be included in a job description:[1]

1. Mission or purpose of the employee's job in broad terms.

2. A list of specific responsibilities.

3. Reservations of authority (such as committing the organization's funds or completing contractual arrangements with outside organizations).

---

[1]From *Putting Management Theories to Work* by Marion S. Kellogg, revised by Irving Burstiner, Ph.D. © 1979. Reprinted by permission of the publisher, Prentice-Hall, Inc., Englewood Cliffs, N.J.

4. Description of working relationships with other positions.

5. Specific objective measures or standards for the work.

6. The assets, contacts, and specialized experience this individual brings to the job and is expected to maintain and develop. These represent the individual's "personal" investment in the organization.

7. The salary range of the position and the way in which both the individual and organizational accomplishment will be judged in determining them.

8. A statement of personal liability in the event of individual or organizational failure, including the effect on salary, employment, and probably future allocation of human and physical resources. (p. 86)

It is most important for workers to have a clear idea of what they are to *accomplish*. That is, ultimately jobs must be described in terms of *outcomes* and not just the behaviors leading to outcomes.

Since systems are not as rational as Kellog and Burstiner's list suggests, it is common that one or more of these elements are left out of any given individual's job description. Indeed, some systems fail to provide even rudimentary job descriptions. Part of the self-defeating arationality of some organizations and institutions is that often enough individuals and units are not sure what is expected of them. Consider the case of the following individual.

EXAMPLE: A woman offered her services as a volunteer in a mental health center. The center was glad to accept her offer but little organizational structure was in place for coordinating the efforts of volunteers. The woman found herself at times the object of an over-whelming number of requests and at other times searching for something to do. The tasks differed widely in seriousness. At one time she would be running messages or getting coffee for staff members and at the next comforting the mother of a boy that had been just arrested for shoplifting. The woman at times felt exhilarated by the work and even the disorganization of the place, but at other times became depressed. Several requests for more structure and direction went unheeded. She finally left, a bit disillusioned about the role of the volunteer.

This woman was a victim of a poorly organized service center. Being socialized into this system meant being socialized into its disorder.

Person Specification

Item 6 on Kellog and Burstiner's list is often called "person specification" and considered separately. That is, many organizations not only use job descriptions to outline roles and responsibilities but also person specifications outlining the kinds of skills and characteristics a person will need to operate successfully in that role. ABC learned about person specification the hard way.

> EXAMPLE: A secretary without some essential skills was hired into a position in ABC Airways. Once she began to perform poorly and her manager began to complain about her performance, the people in the personnel department who had mistakenly hired her moved her to a different position in the organization. In fact, the woman was moved over a dozen times in two years, developed a variety of physical complaints, visited neurologists and psychiatrists, quit but then claimed she had been "pushed out" of the organization, had her case reviewed extensively on two different occasions—one of which was ordered by the president of the company—and finally left with a sizeable separation package. One of the accountants was asked to review the case and estimate the amount of money that had been poured into it. The answer: nearly $300,000.

If there is no person specification, if it is not clear, if it is not clearly related to the role the person is to assume, or if it is ignored, then the organization might well be signing a blank check. The strategy of ABC's human resources department calls for less traditional personnel work and more internal consulting. And so the person specification for the personnel officer position must call for an expanded set of experiences, skills, and assertiveness.

Role Flexibility

There is a trade-off between role clarity and role flexibility. Ideally, a role defines the ways in which a person can be of service to the company or institution or one of the subunits within it. There is often a *range* of ways in which a person can be useful. Although flight attendants cannot fly the plane and although they are there primarily for the sake of safety, there is a range of ways in which they can make the flight more enjoyable for passengers. It is impossible to specify all of these in a job description, and yet the role is clear. Clarity of roles is not the same as rigidity.

Vaill (1980) points out that people often play multiple roles in systems even though they have not been assigned these roles explicitly. He talks about loose boundaries, role creation, and the assumption of authority.

• **Loose Boundaries.** People perform functions outside the stated boundaries of their role. For instance, aides in psychiatric hospitals engage in functions such as listening to patients' problems and giving advice, functions formally relegated to counselors and psychotherapists. People in service industries often find themselves playing a variety of roles.

EXAMPLE: A man checked into a hotel in Washington one wintry night and discovered that there was no clothes rod in the closet. A call to the front desk brought up a maintenance man, who said that he wanted to see this with his own eyes because he had never heard of someone ripping out a clothes rod before. Once he had verified the situation, however, he went into action. He called the front desk, got an upgraded room for the guest, took the luggage to the new room, made sure the guest was settled, apologized for the inconvenience, and delivered a new key. He moved into the needed role quickly and gracefully. The guest was impressed.

This might have been a question of individual initiative. If all staff members of this airline-affiliate hotel are encouraged to cross role boundaries in order to satisfy guests, then it is an outstanding operation indeed.

• **Role Creation.** In order to deliver business outcomes, workers may need to get involved in activities for which no role definition exists. For example, many of ABC's personnel officers acted as internal management and organizational consultants even before this became one of the major categories of service offered by the human resources department. It goes without saying that some people create self-serving rather than institution-serving roles. A university fired a supervisor in the bursar's office because she assumed the role of policy maker, changing the rules on tuition payments to make it more convenient for herself.

- **Assumption of Authority.** Sometimes flexibility means that the members of a system have to risk taking more responsibility than they have authority for (Vaill, 1980):

> The opportunity to accept more responsibility than matching authority has always existed, but in the modern organization increasingly the work will not get done if one is not willing to function with less clear authority than one might like. (p. 26)

Vaill goes on to suggest that this "work-not-done" may well be that on which the very survival of the system depends. For instance, nurses, at legal risk, perform services for patients that are supposed to be performed only by doctors. Hannafin and Witt (1983) enter a plea for an expanded role for school psychologists. They catalog the kinds of system failures that plague schools due to "work-not-done" and suggest that system-level intervention is a natural complement to their individual-level interventions with students and staff. Their research shows that many school psychologists would like to move beyond traditional tester-diagnostician and counselor-therapist roles to the role of internal consultant.

Vaill claims that the best people in organizations, institutions, and communities are role-creative, that is, "endlessly intrigued, challenged, and amused to explore the mutuality, the interplay, and the evolution of self and role" (p. 26). There is, of course, the danger that role creativity might lead to role-inappropriate behavior. This is one of the tensions with which the role-creative person lives. At its best, role flexibility is another instance of the fact that informal dimensions of a system can be both individual- and system-enhancing. The arational ideal—informal, system-enhancing role flexibility— differs from the rational ideal: formally defined roles that are crisp and clear.

Premature Roles

People often play roles in systems before they are ready. At best this can be a system-enhancing form of risk taking. At worst, it can damage the image of an entire unit.

EXAMPLE: The director of human resources for ABC Airways asked his personnel officers to adopt the role of internal organizational consultant before they had been trained as consultants and before line managers had been informed that this new service would be available. Some had already been playing this role and were glad that it was now part of the performance package. Others were excited by the new role and had the common sense and experience to carry it off. A few failed miserably. But the failures got the most publicity.

The world is filled with people playing roles before they have the skills and maturity to carry them off. Witness parenthood. In organizations, the trade-off is often between organizational control and personal creativity.

Role Conflict

Role conflict occurs when an individual or group is identified with two or more individuals or groups that have different and incompatible objectives and values (Dessler, 1976). Expectations do not coincide. For instance, I was hired once to teach one semester in an overseas program of an American university. When I arrived there the tasks outlined went, in my estimation, beyond the tasks discussed with me during contract negotiations. For instance, I found out that I was expected to listen to student tapes and evaluate long papers as part of a comprehensive examination system. Had I known that such tasks were to be part of the job, I would have had second thoughts about accepting the position.

A person can experience role conflict when two or more people to whom he or she relates have different expectations of him or her. For instance, a nurse at times has to choose between the authority of her supervisor and the authority of the doctor. This can lead to stress, dissatisfaction, and lowered productivity. Zawacki (1963) found that role conflict results from the dual hierarchy of hospitals. Those affected respond with hostility to physicians and passive resistance to formal rules.

A high school teacher relates to both students and parents whose goals and values at times conflict. Students are looking for greater freedom, while parents are looking for greater supervision and control. A high school counselor had to deal with the needs the students he or she sees and which may differ from the needs of parents, teachers, and administrators with respect to the student. In the airline industry there can be a conflict between safety requirements and the need for speed and cost effectiveness. ABC mounts an internal and external advertising campaign which states that safety takes precedence over everything else.

Reconceptualizing Roles

I suggest a role exercise that I have found useful in the classroom and which can be adapted to other work settings. I have students write on a piece of paper the two roles found in the classroom: teacher and student. I mention that these are generic roles and ask students to write down the subroles in both the teacher and student package. Under "teacher" they tend to put such things as "coordinator," "appraiser," and "disciplinarian." Under "student" there are traditional roles such as "learner." Then I ask them to draw a line and come up with some more creative and even "wild" roles under each. The results usually challenge the way classrooms are ordinarily structured. For instance, one student in an organizational development course put "convener" under "student." He said, "Usually teachers are the only ones allowed to convene the class. However, this class deals with quality of work life and I am the quality-of-work-life director for my district. Therefore, there seems to be no reason why I could not 'convene' the group or part of it around my experience and expertise." No reason in the world. The use of imagination in reconceptualizing the roles within a company or institution can be a system- and individual-enhancing exercise.

Following are some questions that can be asked to determine whether the division of labor within the organizational unit is contributing to excellence in the delivery of products and services to customers:

- Are all the positions we have in the unit needed, that is, do they actually contribute to business outcomes?
- Which activities now carried out in the unit would, if dropped, make little or no difference? In other words, where is the fat in the unit?
- How do job descriptions indicate the kinds of outcomes or accomplishments expected of the person who holds the position?
- How clear and realistic are these accomplishment-oriented job descriptions?
- To what degree are job descriptions revised as the work changes?
- To what extent do we add or drop positions as the work changes?
- How clear are the person specifications for each job?
- How flexible are the roles? How easily adapted to changing conditions?
- In what ways can the roles in the unit be made more meaningful?
- What do we do up-front to avoid role ambiguity? conflict? overload?

12

Competent Units
with Competent People

It is not enough to have the right units; the units must do the right things. It is not enough to have the right positions and roles; competent and compatible people need to fill these positions and deliver quality products and services to internal and external customers.

COMPETENT UNITS

On the assumption that an organizational unit is needed, what makes it competent? Here is an example of a unit that is considered incompetent.

EXAMPLE: Although there is a corporate training unit located in the human resources department of ABC Airways, its role in the organization has never been that clear. An extremely competent director who replaced a director considered unimaginative and incompetent has been snatched away by another airline after less than two months in office. So the new director of corporate training has been taking stock. Here are some of the facts.

The reputation of the training unit, though beginning to improve under the director hired by another airline, is not good. Although a fledgling management-development program sponsored by corporate training is doing well, its success is being attributed to the external trainers who have designed it and have been delivering it.

Cabin crew services has its own training unit, but its trainers—competent flight attendants showing promise as trainers—receive their training in basic instructional skills from corporate offices, but members of cabin crew services are not happy with this arrangement.

They are seen as a premier training group not only in the airline but in the industry and they feel that the training their trainers get at corporate level is mediocre at best. They are pushing to do all their training under the aegis of cabin crew services.

This is symptomatic of the tack being taken by operations with respect to their training needs. A number of operational divisions have contracted with outside vendors for training and development. For instance, engineering has adopted a nationally recognized quality-assurance training program. Marketing has contracted for a leadership training program. Many training vendors by-pass corporate training entirely and sell their wares directly to line managers. As a result there is no overall coordination of training efforts and no one knows what training, other new director that over the years corporate training had lost touch with the needs and wants of the units it was supposed to serve.

The director of corporate training has been told by the new vice president of human resources to see to it that corporate training "gets its act together." This is part of a larger effort to transform the rather "soft" image of the human resources department itself. It is evident that the corporate training function at ABC needs to be overhauled. A template for the overhaul is also needed.

Since Model A applies, not just to the entire system, but to all the units within the system, it supplies a template for judging whether a unit is competent or not. That is, a unit is competent if it has its business strategy straight, if it "delivers the goods" to its customers, and if its organizational structure, processes, and procedures enable it to operate effectively, efficiently, and humanely. Finally, only effective leadership produces this kind of excellence. ABC Airways is considered to have an excellent cabin-crew training (CCT) unit (quite unlike the corporate training unit). What does this mean concretely?

• **Markets.** CCT understands its internal markets: new crew members, crew members transferring in from other airlines, crew members needing some kind of updating—for instance, flight attendants whose original training had been shortened because of a sudden upswing in market demand—a new category of part-time crew members, and crew members being promoted to supervisory positions. CCT also takes pains to understand the range of felt and prescribed needs of crew members in each of these markets. CCT has also developed an external market. It has established a school that offers its training services on a contract basis to other airlines.

• **Environment.** CCT understands its internal environment and manages it well. For instance, it has had to manage its relationship with the corporate training department, one of the units of the airline that has not yet been updated. The current director of CCT, being politically astute, has managed to get the resources to run its own train-the-trainer program rather than getting poorly trained trainers from the corporate program. And yet because he is willing to act as a covert consultant to the new director of corporate training and has provided the corporate program with other services, he has not turned corporate training into an adversary.

• **Mission.** CCT has a keen understanding of the new strategy of ABC. Its own mission stresses the role CCT plays in delivering a strategy based on service. CCT wants to provide cabin crew operations with flight attendants who are both ready and willing to provide, not just the ordinary in-flight services, but that "something more" that puts ABC at the head of the pack. CCT's aspiration is to be and to be seen as the best cabin-crew training program in the industry.

• **Business Values.** CCT continually focuses on the "put people first" ethic of the airline. It tries to incorporate this philosophy into its own operations and to instill it or rekindle it in flight attendants. Its training programs also stress teamwork and the value of ongoing feedback on quality of service delivery. This links to a corporate strategy of establishing a "culture of feedback" throughout the airline.

• **Major Categories of Training Services.** CCT has a clear idea of the major categories of the services it offers its internal and external customers. Prospective flight attendants receive training in safety, food-service, duty-free sales, problem-solving, and passenger-comfort categories. They are also trained to be sales people for the airline by providing information to passengers on a range of ABC scheduled-flight and tour-package services.

• **Specific Training Accomplishments.** CCT consistently gets feedback from the cabin crew operations department, passengers, and even flight attendants already on the line, veterans who can be quite blase and cynical, that the CCT training programs produce flight attendants that are knowledgeable, self-assured, competent, and caring. Flight attendants come from the courses equipped with the working knowledge, skills, and values needed to deliver high-quality service. CCT has also been commended by the CEO for keeping up to an extremely demanding training timetable in order to keep up with market demand. In all the services it delivers, CCT keeps its eye on the ultimate client, the passenger.

• **Customer Service.** Since flight-attendant trainees are the direct recipients of CCT services, they are CCT's frontline clients. Almost all flight attendants who have gone through the training courses see the training school as something special. They get rigorous training and straight performance-related feedback in a humane and caring atmosphere. They are actually proud of the airline's demanding standards. In carrying out its mission, CCT is also very responsive to the needs of its main internal client, cabin crew operations. For instance, it has willingly put on a crash training program when market research indicated that summer traffic would be much higher than previously predicted.

• **Work Programs.** CCT has reviewed the training programs of all major airlines and has borrowed a range of training approaches that have led to more effective delivery of training results. CCT has hired top-flight training specialists to help revamp its training programs. Current training programs incorporate the best ideas in adult education and experiential learning.

• **Material Resources.** The airline's business plan has allocated the physical and budgetary resources CCT needs to deliver its programs. For instance, the training school has the video equipment needed to provide immediate feedback on a range of customer-service activities. And yet CCT does not squander it resources. The first week of the cabin-crew training program was previously held in a local hotel in order to make new trainees feel special. But a training consultant suggested that the trainees need to be socialized into the realities of the airline as quickly as possible. This meant on-site training right from the start. The resources allocated to hotel training were dropped from the budget.

• **Unit Performance Plan.** CCT has pulled these strategic and operational business factors together in a unit performance plan that establishes priorities linked to the strategic priorities of its parent unit, cabin crew services, and the strategic priorities of the airline itself. This unit plan is the basis for the individual performance plans of everyone working in CCT.

In sum, a competent unit is one that runs its business well. Of course, a competent unit is also one that has its organization straight. If we were to review the organizational structure and procedures of CCT, we would see that this unit has learned how to make its organization serve business outcomes.

Below are some questions that can be asked to determine the competency of the organizational units in a company or institution:

• How well specified is the mission of our unit?
• How well is the mission of our unit integrated with the mission of our parent unit and the overall mission of the company or institution?
• How well is the mission of our unit communicated to those who work in it?
• To what degree does the mission of our unit actually drive the behavior of those who work here?
• How well does our unit know our internal and external customers and their needs?
• How well do we deal with our internal and external customers and their needs?
• What kind of reputation do our products or services have?
• What do our customers say of us?
• What kind of spirit exists in our unit?
• What would we need to do to become an exemplar unit in the organization?

Ultimately, a unit is only as competent as the people that staff it. So a review of the principles pertaining to acquiring, developing, and utilizing human resources is the next order of business.

MANAGING HUMAN RESOURCES

Time after time companies and institutions hire problems and then not only keep them but even promote them. While every organization makes mistakes in hiring from time to time, the best establish human resource policies and procedures to minimize this tendency. More than that, since they really believe that people are their most important resource, they take the next step: they establish a viable human resource management system that includes effective recruitment, development, and appraisal. As Pearson (1987) puts it, they use every opportunity to "muscle-build" the organization by choosing the best people, setting rigorous performance standards, and weeding out poor performers. Staffing and development will be treated in this chapter. Appraisal, since it is an important transaction between workers and their supervisors, will be considered in Chapters 14 (Communication Processes) and 16 (Individual Performance Plans).

STAFFING

Staffing includes attracting promising prospects, assessing their compatibility and ability to perform, and selecting the most promising candidates.

Attracting Promising Prospects

The best companies and institutions don't merely take what they get. They look for the best. This calls for imagination in self-presentation. The first question is: Are we the kind of company or institution that the best prospects would want to join? Second: What do we need to do to catch the attention of the kind of people we want to recruit? Some institutions offer a challenge. A magazine ad calling for people to join the Peace Corps showed a picture of a South American village before the arrival of Peace Corps workers. On the following page there was a picture of the same village a year after the Peace Corps arrived. It was the very same picture. The ad, while cautioning prospective workers not to expect miracles, went on to spell out how the Peace Corps members themselves would be challenged and changed for the better by working abroad. ABC Airways has been pursuing a program of organizational renewal and excellence for about five years. The image of the airline is currently excellent. They draw applicants of the highest caliber.

Since in our society many, if not most, jobs are obtained by word of mouth, an organization should ask itself: What kind of emissaries do we have out there sharing their enthusiasm about working for this company? The personnel board of a large Catholic diocese was shocked to learn from a study that many priests tended to discourage young men from following in their footsteps. An organization probably gets the kinds of prospects it deserves. Winners tend to attract winners; losers tend to attract losers.

Assessing Prospects

Organizations hire problems because their assessment procedures are poor. They select people who are incompetent. Or they select competent people without considering their compatibility.

EXAMPLE: The director of a health care center hired a man to head up the alcoholic unit. The latter was certainly qualified in terms of both credentials and references. A couple of months after the director hired him, she sought the help of a consultant to find some way, legally, to fire him. The new person was competent but hampered productivity by doing a range of things that seriously interfered with the quality of work life in the unit. He was arrogant and politicized almost everything he did. Behind the scenes he tried to sabotage the "clinical ladder" career-development program the director of the clinic was promoting. The director, blinded by the testimonials to this person's competence, had not read between the lines in the letters of recommendation and had made no further efforts to learn anything about his employment background. She later admitted that her interview with him had been a social event, superficial, and grossly inadequate.

The director of the center joins a long line of people who, because of sloppy assessment procedures, have hired competent trouble. On the other hand, ABC Airways is rigorous in its choice of flight attendants. Candidates learn that being accepted for the training program does not assure employment. The training program itself is the second phase of assessment.

Assessment procedures are important not just for recruiting but also for classifying, promoting, transferring, demoting, and terminating employees. The aim of this process is clear: making a decision as to whether the prospect has the requisite working knowledge, skills, compatibility, and relevant personal qualities. The critical issue here is knowing what is being looked for, that is, knowing exactly what "requisite" means. Therefore, meaningful assessment of prospects depends on clarity of mission, products or services, work programs, roles, tasks, and responsibilities. If the elements of Model A are not in order, then relevant assessment procedures will not be in order.

Establishing Criteria. The purpose of an assessment is to determine whether the prospect:

- Has the working knowledge needed for the job;
- Has the skills needed for the job;
- Has the capacity and the will to be trained, if he or she does not currently have the requisite working knowledge and skills;
- Is attracted to the organization and interested in the job;
- Is compatible with the mission of the company or institution and with the mission of the particular unit of which he or she will be a member;
- Is compatible with the team with which he or she will be working;
- Will contribute to, or at least not detract from, the quality of life of those who work in the system; or
- In a word, has all the personal attributes and skills called for by the person specification.

The truth is that people are chosen for all sorts of reasons different from and even in opposition to these criteria. Covert criteria include good looks, aggressiveness, political and social contacts within the organization, and compatibility with the covert, but dysfunctional, culture of the system. For instance, a lawyer may be chosen for the legal department of a large corporation because of her conservative life style. The covert culture of the organization requires that "women know their place." If interviewers do not carefully outline just what they are looking for and how they will find it, unnamed qualities fill the gap and are unconsciously looked for in applicants.

Assessment Instruments and Strategies. We are all familiar with the ordinary ways of assessing prospects: standard or specialized application blanks, written tests, including personality tests, performance tests, interviews, physical examinations, check lists, references, background investigations, and probationary periods (boot camp, novitiate experiences). The right mix of instruments and strategies can be chosen only if the strong and weak points of each of the above methods are understood. For instance, consider references: "Getting references of any value from a previous employer. . . is like filching trade secrets from the Soviet Union. At the drop of an unflattering word, employees will haul an employer into court" (Kleinfield, 1982, p.4). This does not mean that getting references safely is not possible; it means that it must be done judiciously and in ways that protect the rights of prospective system members.

Interviewing. Interviewing is the most widely used method of assessing the qualifications of a prospect, even though the way that it is ordinarily carried out makes it neither a reliable nor a valid assessment tool (Guion, 1976; Dunnette & Borman, 1979; Schmitt, 1976). Interviewers need to work from a recruitment model and develop competency in interviewing skills.

EXAMPLE: In one company there was a great deal of dissatisfaction with the recruitment division of the personnel department. The decision was made to decentralize the function. Managers would get their own recruits. However, since line managers possessed no training in recruitment, the consultant suggested that incompetence was not being managed but merely redeployed.

Even skilled interviewers are subjected to their own biases and the political pressures around them. Sometimes it helps to interview in twos. It is more difficult to be seduced by my biases if I am being watched as well as the interviewee. When I suggested that we add interviewing to the assessment process in assessing applicants to a doctoral program in clinical psychology, one of my colleagues suggested that it was a waste of time. However, upon returning from one of the first interviews he had conducted, he said: "On paper this candidate seemed outstanding. Without an interview I would have chosen him instantly, but a fifteen-minute interview made it absolutely clear that this person would never make a good clinical psychologist."

Interviews are two-way streets. The organization is choosing the applicant, but the applicant is also choosing the organization. Wanous (1980) suggests that "realistic job previews" should be part of the recruitment process. A realistic job preview provides applicants with information about both the positive and negative aspects of a job. Wanous's research showed that such previews can help newcomers develop more realistic job expectations and can lead to a lower turnover rate.

Performance Samples. Sampling actual performance is a promising, if expensive, form of assessment. The director of the management-development program for a large organization never hires trainers without seeing them in action. Applicants are invited to conduct a training seminar. The "trainees" are trainers in the management-development unit and volunteer managers who know what effective training is like. The session is videotaped. After the session, the applicant reviews the tape alone and then meets with the director of the unit to discuss both the strengths and weaknesses demonstrated in the session. He or she is also given written feedback from the "trainees." The process is expensive, but not nearly as expensive as hiring an incompetent and/or incompatible trainer.

THE DEVELOPMENT OF HUMAN RESOURCES

Development includes enculturation, education and training, effective utilization of human resources, and career development.

Enculturation

Some companies and institutions choose excellent people and then fail to introduce or enculturate them effectively into the system. The way people spend their first days or weeks in an organization can set the tone for their participation in the system.

EXAMPLE: John was hired as a pilot for one of ABC Airways' low-cost competitors. He soon found that he was working in an organization with a climate of suspicion between management and pilots. The pilots' group was a hodgepodge: veterans who had not participated in a bitter strike, veterans who had, newer pilots, some of whom had become disenchanted by their lower wages, and a mixture of pilots from three other airlines that had been recently acquired. Some of these pilots were angry because they had been demoted and their pay had been slashed. Because there was no enculturation program, John learned the ropes haphazardly from his fellow pilots. The result? John learned to be on guard, with one wary eye on management, another on dissatisfied colleagues.

This is hardly a picture of a professional joining a group of colleagues committed to the mission of their unit and the overall mission and strategy of the company. Companies and institutions with successful enculturation programs come up with creative answers to the following questions:

- What are the needs of the system with respect to the newcomer?
- What are the needs of the newcomer with respect to the system?
- What outcomes or accomplishments related to both productivity and quality of work life constitute initial integration?
- What programs can be developed that will help ensure that newcomers become both productive and at home as quickly as possible?

Many companies and institutions conduct "orientation" sessions or talks that are dull and meaningless. They are canned programs that perhaps meet some bureaucratic and administrative needs, but they certainly do little for the new employee. Excellent companies and institutions do not leave integration to chance.

Training

The term *training* will be used here to indicate both the acquisition or expansion of working knowledge and the acquisition or improvement of skills. Unfortunately, a great deal of money spent on training is misspent. For instance, as Goldstein (1980) points out, there is a strong belief that training in and of itself results in better job performance and increased productivity. This is simply not the case. Often little is done to find out whether any given training program actually does contribute to productivity.

Training programs and tools are meaningless unless training needs have been assessed and training goals specified. The aim of training is not "to train people" nor is it even "people trained" (see Gilbert, 1978). Rather it is the acquisition or improvement of performance-related working knowledge and skills. Gilbert claims that much training done is both ineffective and inefficient. Since training is expensive, it should take place only if an affirmative answer can be given to both of two questions:

1. Are the skills relevant to productivity and/or quality of life?

2. Does this particular person lack this set of skills?

Many training programs train people in skills that are either irrelevant or already possessed by the trainee. Many people that are trained in order to become more productive would benefit more, at a lower price, from accurate information about what to do. Gilbert (1978) asks the following hard-nosed questions about training:[1]

1. Has training been installed to meet a proven and measured performance need?

2. Are there performance measures to show that training is working for us?

3. Are the measures taken independently, or do we have only our training staff's word that training works?

---

[1]From *Human Competence: Engineering Worthy Performance* (pp. 238-239) by T.F. Gilbert, 1978. New York: McGraw-Hill. Reprinted by permission.

4. Is exemplary performance the standard for training? [Exemplary performance is the performance of the best worker, with the proper incentives, working "smart" rather than hard.] And does the trainee reach the standard?

5. Are the people in charge of training competent, or is training relegated to those who just aren't good at other jobs?

6. How long is our training, formal or OJT [on the job training]? How long does it take a trainee to become a top performer on the job? If it takes more than, say, a month or two, we are probably missing great opportunities.

7. What are the true costs of our training, formal or OJT? There is little excuse not to know.

8. Are training costs budgeted?

9. What is an estimate of the value we are getting for our training?

10. Are our course lengths arbitrary or are they determined only by the time required for training?

11. Do we have access to really expert training development skills?

12. Do our training people know how to conduct a performance audit? (pp. 238-239)

Training can suffer from the tyranny of work programs; that is, clear and specific goals related to clear and specific performance needs are not established and training is thrown at trainees in the hope that it will do some good. If this is the case, the training department takes on a kind of functional autonomy that militates against the better interests of the total organization.

This does not mean that there should be a bias against training. On the contrary, as Peters and Waterman (1982) state, the best organizations provide ample opportunities for training and development. It is an essential part of "muscle building" the organization. Failure in essential training can lead to failure of the entire enterprise.

EXAMPLE: A friend of mine entered a hospital for a minor operation, his first encounter with surgery. After the admissions procedures, the desk clerk said, "One of our volunteers will take you to your room." My friend turned to the volunteer, who—without a word and with a somewhat impassive look on her face—started walking toward the elevator. She maintained her silence in the elevator and said nothing, in fact, until they were in the hospital room. She gestured toward some pamphlets that dealt with general hospital procedures and with the kind of operation my friend was to undergo. Finally she said, "The resident should be in later this afternoon to examine you." With that, she left.

Here was a person of good will who did not have the basic working knowledge and skills needed to carry our her tasks effectively. If she had done her work well, my friend's anxiety and concerns would have been allayed a bit and he would have felt welcome in the institution. However, by the time he reached his room, he felt *worse* than when he first came through the entrance of the hospital. The volunteer could have been helped, through a simple training program, to understand how patients feel as they enter the hospital and what simple things might be done to help them adjust to their new surroundings.

ABC not only provides excellent training for its pilots and flight attendants, but it also evaluates training outcomes. "Handsome is as handsome does" is the motto of these two training programs. It is quite clear by the end of the training programs whether trainees have the requisite skills or not, but the trainees also know that they will continue to receive feedback on the line. Training outcomes are proved on the line. Catalanello and Kirkpatrick (1968) surveyed 154 companies with respect to how they assessed the effectiveness of training. Most (77 percent) said that they used reactions of trainees rather than determining whether job-related learning had taken place or whether on-the-job-performance improved. The problem with education and training is the cultural tendency to see them as good things in and of themselves. This is one form of arationality that is extremely difficult to manage.

Keeping the Best System Members

It is a mistake to take people for granted once they have settled into the system. One sign that effective development procedures are in place is that the best people stay and flourish. Personnel turnover can have both a positive and a negative side. In a positive sense, it can mean that new blood is coming into the organization. These newcomers may be people who want to learn and do more, people with fresh hopes, new ideas, contagious enthusiasm, and refreshing vigor. In a backhanded way, turnover can also mean that selection mistakes are being remedied. However, turnover can be a sign that things are going wrong. It means that good or at least adequate people are opting out of the system. Turnover can be costly in a variety of ways. New people need to be trained. There can be confusion as new people learn the ropes. High turnover can affect morale, that is, people can begin asking themselves what is wrong with a system that cannot retain its members, especially its good members.

How does an organization keep its good members? The answer is simple in theory, more difficult in practice. The principle is this: People tend to stay in a system until the incentives to leave it outweigh the incentives to stay.

EXAMPLE: The new director was given the job of turning ABC's corporate training unit around. However, his superiors failed to understand either his skills or his ambition. He was in the new job for only a couple of months when he was hired away by another airline. The managerial challenge of a position in a different international airline was more in line with his skills, and the financial rewards were more attractive. Everyone thought that his leaving was a great loss, but none of his supervisors had ever sat down with him to map out a viable career-development strategy.

People stay in distasteful jobs until the punitive dimensions outweigh the agony of searching for and changing to a new job. Or they stay in decent jobs until better ones come along.

A Human Assets Framework

The best organizations have some kind of human assets framework that enables managers and supervisors to stay in touch with the individual needs of workers and manage them according to these needs. Odiorne (1984) adapts a "portfolio analysis" framework, assessing human assets as one might assess financial assets. Figure 12-1 presents a version of the portfolio grid.

The following four "positions" are indicated in the grid, though there could be many more.

• **The Star.** In the northeast corner, we have people who are very productive, but who still have unused talent. These are the stars. Stars need autonomy but they also need to be monitored.

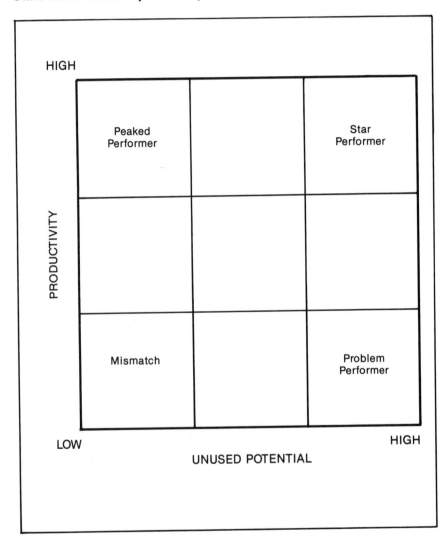

Figure 12-1. Human-Assets Framework

• **The Peaked Performer.** In the northwest corner, we have people who are very productive, but they are using all the talent they have. Since they have no further *unused* potential with respect to the tasks for which they are responsible (though they may have unused potential for other tasks), to promote them or give them more responsibility would be a case of the "Peter Principle" (Peter and Hull, 1970), that is, giving people more and more responsibility until they finally settle into a position in which they are incompetent.

• **The Problem Performer.** In the southeast corner, we have people who have unused potential, but who, for whatever reasons, are not using it. Therefore, their productivity is low. These are the problem performers.

• **The Mismatch.** Finally, in the southwest corner, we have people who are not productive because they do not seem to have the kinds of abilities needed for the positions they are in or because they are not committed to the mission of the unit or the company. Since it would be unkind to suppose that they are without talent and motivation for other jobs, they are given the title of "mismatch."

While a simplistic application of such a framework would do more harm than good, still good managers and supervisors have some kind of formal or informal framework that help them understand and assess the overall mix of human resources in their units and the strengths and weaknesses of each individual. Such frameworks can be used as cynical tools to help managers profit from "workhorses," get rid of "deadwood," and threaten "laggards," but in the best companies and institutions they are used to help managers and supervisors not only assess the overall status of the human capital of the organization but also manage people according to their needs (see Pfeiffer, 1986).

Effective Utilization of Human Resources

All of us are aware of organizations in which the talents of those who work there are not being fully utilized. These can be deadening places in which to work. The poor utilization of human resources is more likely a managerial than a worker problem. Lippitt (1979, p. 309) describes human resource utilization as "putting the right heads together, at the right time, for the right task, with the right support to get a particular job done." Lippitt believes that the first step in using human resources intelligently is identifying just what these resources are. Just because someone is hired or chosen to do one task does not mean that he or she does not have the capability of doing others. He suggests that a system would do well to compile a "human resource directory" in which individuals would be listed alphabetically with a rundown on their abilities, and also abilities would be listed alphabetically with the names of those who possess them.

> EXAMPLE: The director of human resources at ABC has a chart that lists all the professionals working in his unit. Across the top are listed all the types of skills and resources that might be needed for a wide range of projects. He places checks after each name, indicating which person has which abilities or skills. Then when he needs people for a special assignment or wants to put together a task force or project team, he merely glances at the chart.

Such a human-resource directory needs, of course, to be kept up to date. For instance, when computer programmers receive further education or training, either formal or on-the-job, care should be taken to add new aptitudes.

Merely knowing what people's abilities are is meaningless unless there is access to them. Lippitt suggests that in some, if not most, systems, there is a cultural taboo against asking for help, that is, calling others in as consultants or co-workers on a project. He describes one company in which all staff members have a resource directory of their colleagues. One item on the agenda every month is to review how they have used each other during the past month. The administrator rewards and recognizes those who ask for help. What is rewarded is not the cry for help, but the problem solving and increased productivity that come from colleague consultation.

The Ongoing Development of Human Resources

When I first began going to the dentist who currently takes care of my dental needs, while I was comforted to see up-to-date popular magazines in the waiting room, I was even more heartened to see professional magazines with a used look in the inner office. My conversations with him certainly gave me the impression that he was staying current with the latest in technology and that this would benefit me. The fact that he attended one or two professional conferences a year reinforced this impression.

Ongoing development is both an individual and an organizational concern. There are two issues: keeping up with one's field and career development within the particular organization. The latter needs to be a part of the overall organizational human resource strategy. The world is filled with people who feel they should be moving forward in their respective companies and institutions, but "forward" is usually defined as "upward." In a world in which downsizing is the rage, this presents all sorts of complications. The growth of the Forties, Fifties, and Sixties set up expectations that cannot currently be met. New units and new positions were established, and development in the minds of many was tied almost exclusively to promotions and the financial rewards that go with it. In the long run, this was an unrealistic approach to career development. The problem is that this kind of unreality has become part of the corporate culture of many companies and institutions. What is needed is a variety of creative approaches to career development tied to financial realities and organizational needs.

Here are some questions than can help an organization or a unit focus on the management of human resources:

- What kind of organizational human-resources strategy do we have?
- How well is that strategy communicated to and implemented in each organizational unit?
- How well do we recruit people for this unit?
- To what degree do we get people who are competent? eager? compatible with the mission of the unit? with the teams in the unit?
- How well do we enculturate or socialize people into the unit?
- To what degree do we have the right people for the right jobs?
- What do we do with our problem people?

- What do we do with people who have peaked and are growing restless?
- How well do we manage our star performers?
- How well are managers and supervisors equipped with the kinds of coaching and counseling skills needed to help problem performers?
- What problems do we have, such as turnover, that indicate that we have staffing problems?
- How well do we develop our workers through training or other experiences?
- What are we doing with workers whose skills are outdated?
- What do we do with productive but "difficult" people?
- What is our current career-development strategy?

13

Teamwork:
The Reintegration of Labor

While, as we have seen in Chapter 11, it is absolutely necessary to divide up the work of the system, it is just as essential to reintegrate it at the service of business outcomes. "There's the rub," as the poet says. Cooperative and collaborative *relationships* between and among individuals, between and among groups, and between and among departments—relationships that serve business outcomes—are one of the hallmarks of successful companies and institutions. Cooperation and collaboration are not the same thing. Cooperation involves a sharing of the work, while collaboration involves a sharing of power or authority. The quality of relationships within an organization can affect business outcomes in major ways. Relationships include:

- Individual to individual: An ABC manager acts as a mentor to a subordinate who shows a great deal of promise.

- Individual to group: An ABC marketing manager helps her team brainstorm ways of counteracting a downturn in North Atlantic business following a series of terrorist incidents.

- Individual to organization: A member of the ABC human resources department acts as an internal consultant to a reorganization of the information services department.

- Unit to individuals: The cabin crew self-help group offers telephone and walk-in counseling services to all flight attendants.

- Unit to unit: ABC's information services department works closely with the frequent-flyer program unit and reservations to establish special services for frequent business travelers.

- Unit to organization: ABC's human resources planning unit helps the executive team make staffing decisions related to the strategic plan.

SEGMENTALISM

Kanter (1983) suggests that one of the principal reasons that companies and institutions fall short of excellence is the "segmentalism" that plagues most organizations:[1]

> I call it "segmentalism" because it is concerned with compartmentalizing actions, events, and problems and keeping each piece isolated from the others. Segmentalist approaches see problems as narrowly as possible, independently of their context, independently of their connections to any other problems. Companies with segmentalist cultures are likely to have segmented structures: a large number of compartments walled off from one another—department from department, level above from level below, field office from headquarters, labor from management, or men from women. Only the minimum number of exchanges takes place at the boundaries of segments; each slice is assumed to stand or fall rather independently of any other anyway, so why *should* they need to cooperate? Segmentalism assumes that problems can be solved when they are carved into pieces and the pieces assigned to specialists who work in isolation. Even innovation itself can become a specialty in segmentalist systems—something given to the R&D department to take care of so that no one else has to worry about it. (p. 28)

Isolationism and empire building instead of system-enhancing integration in the subunits of a corporation or institution constitute one of the main forms of corporate arationality. Obviously there can be degrees of segmentalism. It can even happen that there are isolated individuals with a "segmentalist" mentality working in companies or institutions with teamwork cultures. While all relationships are

---

[1]From *Change Masters: Innovation for Productivity in the American Corporation.* Copyright © 1983 by Rosabeth Moss Kanter. Reprinted by permission of Simon & Schuster, Inc.

important, the focus here will be on interunit partnerships and teamwork and the fostering of teams within work units. Teamwork is the
opposite of and the antidote to segmentalism.

INTERUNIT TEAMWORK

Do the units in this company collaborate to deliver better products
and services to customers? There are some institutions with such a
history of segmentalism that innovative teamwork between units is
almost inconceivable. Universities, with their untouchable departmental system, are as segmented as any system can be.

> EXAMPLE: The psychology and sociology departments at a large ur-
> ban university, goaded by a few faculty members in each department,
> had a historic meeting to review ways in which the two could co-
> operate. Speeches were made to the effect that the age of inter-
> disciplinary research and projects was at hand. The only decision made
> before the meeting dissolved into a nice social gathering was to meet
> again "soon." It was the last meeting the two departments had, and
> that was over fifteen years ago.

In one Midwest state a university was founded on a policy of interdisciplinary research and teaching. Faculty members were not hired
unless they espoused an interdisciplinary approach. I did not follow
the fortunes of this institution, but some ten years later one of its
administrators ended up in a course I was teaching. He told me that
now the university was "just like all the rest." It is not that a radi-
cally interdisciplinary approach was flawed. Rather the prevalent
culture in American universities ultimately prevailed. Faculty
members do not join universities to become members of teams.

The following example describes a mixture of public and private
enterprise.

> EXAMPLE: The Federal Asset Disposition Association (FADA) was
> established in 1985 by the Federal Home Loan Bank Board to help
> the Federal Savings and Loan Insurance Corporation (FSLIC) manage
> soured loans and foreclosed properties. FSLIC pays FADA fees for the
> latter's services. Over 80 percent of FADA's portfolio is in defaulted
> real-estate loans. FSLIC itself has its hands full attending to the over

300 savings and loan associations that are dangerously weak. Before the establishment of FADA, FSLIC liquidated the assets of failed savings and loan associations through its own stretched staff and contractors. The fact that FADA, a semi-private institution, hired real-estate professionals at salaries higher than those at FSLIC irked many of the civil servants there. The two agencies routinely disagree over how to manage the assets of failed savings and loan associations.

This infighting has apparently escalated. According to a *Business Week* article ("Feuding," 1987), an FSLIC receiver charged that FADA gets "exorbitant" fees, regularly misses deadlines, and may be superfluous since it subcontracts much of its work:

> In the report, FADA itself listed 20 "troublesome areas" in its relationship with FSLIC, including "extreme difficulty" in obtaining FSLIC files, causing FADA to miss some deadlines. . . . FADA is apparently in no position to pick out easy-to-market assets to make its batting average more impressive. Instead, it is assigned assets by its brethren at the FSLIC and generally gets those having complex financial structures. . . . If this quasi-private effort to solve a public problem is to succeed, FADA must shake off the distractions of bureaucratic haggling and show that it can indeed move effectively, and fast, in a tough real estate market. (p. 116)

Hindsight is useful here. Many of the problems that plague the relationship between FSLIC and FADA were built in from the beginning. The lessons are clear. First, when tasks are divided, care should be taken to examine the consequences of the division—the problems that are likely to arise versus the benefits to be reaped. Second, coordinating mechanisms for managing these problems should be established from the beginning and not just when the problems arise.

On the other hand, ABC Airways is exploring ways of increasing teamwork in order to deliver better services to its passengers. For instance, the airline is doing everything it can to reduce delays at major airports. It goes without saying that some causes of delay, such as weather, are beyond its control. However, some delays are caused by a lack of teamwork among units. In order to get a plane away from the gate on time, there must be collaboration among check-in services, baggage handlers, fueling services, plane cleaners, catering, boarding services, the cabin-crew team, and the flight-deck team.

The services provided by each of these units are links in a chain. Failure at any point can delay a flight. Brief weekly meetings are held with representatives from each of these units to discuss issues of mutual concern. Furthermore, ABC is increasing efforts to cooperate with key units of the airports themselves. For instance, it has been able to help in redesigning access roads to cut down on congestion. Late arrival of passengers has been significantly reduced at two key airports.

Interunit teamwork is, ideally, not just an exercise in problem solving but also a source of system-enhancing innovation. An organizational studies department (OSD) in one university is making attempts to practice what it preaches. It wants to model leadership in managing its internal environment. Its aim is to be proactive in establishing and cultivating the kinds of relationships that will benefit itself, other departments, and the university itself. Here are some examples:

• **Foreign Student Office.** Collaborative problem solving with this office has significantly reduced delays experienced by foreign students in getting information on things such as housing and in processing papers needed to get visas. OSD helped the foreign student office streamline many of its procedures.

• **Media Services.** One of the OSD faculty members made some tapes that proved to be a success in the business videotape market. Media services was quite proud of its part in this venture. It helped OSD make an advertising video that was used to attract high-quality prospects.

• **Anthropology Department.** OSD uses one of its faculty members to teach a course on organizational culture. OSD is also helping the anthropology department develop an applied anthropology program.

• **School of Education.** There was some bad blood between OSD and the School of Education. Some members of the latter resisted establishment of the OSD program because they wanted to do it themselves. Once established, OSD actively sought the collaboration of the School of Education and the department of communications in establishing an organizational effectiveness consultancy service.

• **Maintenance Department.** Its services are critical for the many conferences and workshops OSD puts on every year. Early on, the director of OSD met with the director of maintenance and asked in what ways they might collaborate. The director of maintenance was floored by the upbeat nature of the meeting. He had never before been asked about collaboration, and the relationship between maintenance and other units in the university had been either neutral or adversarial.

OSD saw the need to capitalize on other key relationships— with the graduate school to which it directly reported, with the office of continuing education with its myriad outreach possibilities, and with the graduate program review board which evaluates all graduate programs and which reviews the feasibility of new Ph.D. programs.

The following are some questions that can be asked about the quality of interunit teamwork:

• How well do different units work with one another to increase productivity?
• What "empires" have we let develop?
• What significant partnerships have been established with key units and what further partnerships need to be developed?
• To what degree does interunit competition, jealousy, or politics interfere with productivity?
• To what degree does interunit behavior actually decrease productivity?
• In what ways does a spirit of interunit teamwork permeate the organization?
• What innovative forms of collaboration can be developed between functions?

ESTABLISHING EFFECTIVE TEAMS WITHIN UNITS

One disturbing study (Knaus et al., 1986) provides evidence that effective teamwork can, literally, make a difference between life and death. The focus of the study was the intensive-care units of thirteen hospitals. All hospitals had similar technical capabilities in these units but differed in organization, staffing, commitment to teaching, research, and education. The study showed that the intensive-care unit of one hospital (Hospital 1) had a lower death rate than expected. Whereas sixty-nine deaths during the time of the study would have been normal, only forty-one deaths actually occurred. At the other end of the continuum, the intensive-care unit of another hospital (Hospital 13) had 58 percent more deaths than expected. All hospitals in the study had similar technical capabilities and used invasive monitoring, ventilator therapy, and other specialized intensive-care treatment with similar frequency.

"Hospital 1 showed showed a consistent, coordinated response to patients' needs and a division of responsibility among physicians and nurses that precluded many problems" (p. 416). On the other hand, Hospital 13

> had no dedicated unit physician staff to direct admission, discharge, or treatment policy. . . . It also lacked a comprehensive nursing organization. . . . Admitting physicians and unit nursing staff communicated poorly. No policy was established for routine discussion of patient treatment, and there was no direct coordination of staff capabilities with clinical demands. Frequent disagreements about the ability of the nursing staff to treat additional patients occurred, and there was an atmosphere of distrust. During the study, there were also staff shortages that necessitated care by nurses who were not trained in the intensive-care unit. (pp. 415-416)

The problems of Hospital 13 probably go beyond ineffective teamwork, but the data suggests that ineffective teamwork was central to its low standing.

The usefulness of teams in companies and institutions is beyond question. Here is an example of an ad hoc team or task force (Guest, 1986):[2]

> In one of Xerox plants, the team concept has been embraced completely. Not only has the management structure been simplified, but. . .the shop floor is made up of teams meeting every week to solve problems, many of which were traditionally handled by separate support and staff services. With the cooperation of the union, an eight-person Study-Action Team (including workers, an engineer, and a manager) was turned loose for six months with no other duties than to look at the plant from top to bottom. Its explicit purpose was to come up with ideas to improve quality and delivery performance and to lower costs. Major recommendations were made, including the creation of self-managing work teams, new work procedures, new production techniques, and computer systems. Within a year, a half million dollars was saved in excess of a 3.7 million dollar target. (p. 65)

Note that the creation of self-managing teams was one of the outcomes of the work of this task force.

Casey Stengel, the legendary manager of the New York Yankees, once said: "It's easy to get the players. Gettin'em to play together, that's the hard part." In business and institutions, it is not always that easy even to get the right people, much less to get them to work together. Again, the ideal is clear: individuals within departments working in ad hoc or ongoing teams *when interdependence is called for*, accomplishing together what they could not accomplish as effectively working apart. Teamwork is not an end in itself; it needs to serve both productivity and quality of work life. In the subunits within excellent companies and institutions there are two things:

1. An overall spirit of cooperation and collaboration; people value partnerships and teamwork;

2. Actual partnerships—formal or informal, ad hoc or permanent—as they are needed to increase productivity and deliver business outcomes.

There is a vast literature on team building. Some consultants seem to offer team building as a panacea for all the woes a company or

---

[2]© 1986 by the Regents of the University of California. Reprinted from the *California Management Review*, Vol. 28, No. 4. By permission of The Regents.

institution is experiencing. For some, team building is a social-emotional venture; for others, it is a productivity tool. It is obvious from what has been said up to this point that team building is not a panacea. Team building is an organizational intervention that must be based on effective strategic and operational business factors. If the company or institution has the wrong strategy or has a history of poor customer relationships, then mere team building is not the answer, unless team building is interpreted so broadly as to include all the elements of Model A.

PRINCIPLES OF EFFECTIVE TEAMWORK

In many ways, an effective team is no different from an effective company, institution, agency, subunit, or project. The principles of Model A apply to all. A brief review of some of the main principles of team effectiveness will bear this out (see Dyer, 1987; Janis & Mann, 1977; Kormanski & Mozenter, 1987; Likert, 1961, 1967; Johnson, 1986). Some of the principles focus on the business outcomes of the work of the team, while others deal with the kinds of relationships and attitudes that facilitate these outcomes.

1. **Choose people who are compatible with the mission of the team and its members.** A newly-formed research-and-development unit of a small chemical company chose its members exclusively for their skills. The result: endless interpersonal and policy squabbles. Proper working knowledge and skills are needed for team membership, but they do not suffice.

2. **Remain focused on internal and external customers and their needs.** Do not get lost in teamwork for its own sake. One advertising section of the ABC Airways marketing group got so caught up in its own creativity that its "cuteness" actually turned customers off.

3. **Establish a mode of operating.** Make sure the team knows how it is to work as a team. This means clarifying roles, responsibilities, and procedures within the team. When team members go their separate ways, make sure that each knows what he or she is to accomplish and the time frame. Have team members clarify the assumptions and values on which their work is to be based.

4. **Coordinate individual efforts.** If team members are to interrelate effectively, their efforts need to be coordinated. Team assignments on an ABC human resources department task force to establish a comprehensive process for identifying and developing high-potential managers were not clear. The result: reduplication of effort, uncompleted tasks, and a missed deadline. The team leader is conducting an orchestra and coaching a team and is responsible for the "care and feeding" of the team.

5. **Make sure that outcomes of group efforts (products or services to be delivered) are clear.** Volvo assembly teams produce automobiles. On the other hand, team meetings often produce nothing. Currently all meetings in ABC must have not only an agenda but a list of meeting *outcomes*. Minutes are limited to "actionable items." Teams are mini-systems in need of a mission, specific outcomes, and clear work programs.

6. **Give teams both responsibilities and the authority needed to execute them.** ABC had a history of establishing "fact-finding" task forces. They scrapped this approach and began to set up task forces only if they could be given some kind of executive power. Team spirit will disappear if its outputs are not used.

7. **Balance team effort with individual effort.** Work in teams only when it leads to more creative, effective, and efficient delivery of outcomes. Group brainstorming sessions in the ABC marketing group are always preceded by individual brainstorming. The group hits the ground running. Do not let teams swallow up "intrapreneurs" (Pinchot, 1985); do not let intrapreneurs destroy team effort.

8. **Do not squash individual contributions.** Let team members have a say in establishing goals and specifying outcomes. Listen to individuals, especially when they dissent. Do not stifle individual contributions. Avoid "group think." One of ABC's marketing efforts fell flat. It was a poor idea but came from the director of marketing. The sole dissenter actually left the team. Group think prevailed. Surface conflicts and use them to clarify and improve mission, work programs, and outcomes.

9. **Foster the kind of supportive climate that contributes to both improved quality of outcomes and quality of work life.** The members of ABC's cabin-crew training unit love coming to work. While work outcomes are the major source of their satisfaction, this is aided and abetted by mutual support, camaraderie, recognition of efforts and success by higher management, and opportunities for self-development. Reward the team for its accomplishments; recognize individual efforts that contribute in special ways to outcomes.

10. **Get expert help outside the team as needed; do not make the assumption that the team has all the resources within itself.** Outsiders can help teams discover blind spots. As mentioned earlier, ABC's cabin-crew training unit hired professional consultants to help revamp its training programs. However, the team should first decide what it wants to accomplish and then ask experts to help develop optional ways of getting there.

11. **Engage in onging evaluation of both team outcomes and individual contributions to outcomes.** Do not assume that teams are doing well or that they are still needed. In a large development bank, a team was put together to study the impact of a lending policy on the use of energy resources in developing countries. In the meeting in which their conclusions were being discussed with the bank's president, he mused out loud, "I wonder what impact this policy would have on transportation systems in Africa." Months later a huge (and expensive) report was delivered to the president, who had forgotten all about his aside.

The following are some questions that can be asked about teamwork within each unit of a company or institution:

- To what degree does a spirit of teamwork permeate our unit?
- How well can each member of the unit answer this question: In what ways can I cooperate/collaborate with other individuals or other units in order to get the work of the unit done?
- In what ways do we underuse teamwork in getting our work done?

- In what ways do we overuse teamwork at the expense of efficiency and effectiveness?
- When people do work in teams, how well is their work coordinated?
- In what ways does our teamwork enhance business outcomes?
- What do we do about nonteam players?
- What do we do about players who are overly dependent on the team?
- What kind of balance is there between teamwork and individual effort?
- To what degree do we use quality circles or some other form of intraunit collaborative problem solving and innovation development?

14

Communication Processes

If people are to relate well and establish effective teams, they must communicate well. Effective communication is the lifeblood of the system, the energizer, the productivity enhancer. Communication breathes life into relationships in organizations, institutions, and communities. In this section we deal with the kinds of interunit and interpersonal communication and transactions that are needed to make "all the above"—that is, all that has been said about both business and organizational factors—work.

Communication can be defined as the exchange of messages between individuals or system units for the purpose of creating common understandings. For instance, a mechanic at ABC Airways tells his manager that he feels so overloaded with work that the quality of his work is suffering. He believes that other mechanics are taking short cuts that endanger safety. If the message gets through, he and his manager have a common understanding of an issue of utmost importance to the functioning of the airline.

Communication need not be verbal. For instance, the way mechanics look as they go about their work should give the manager enough cues to know that something is going wrong. Not only individuals but also units within organizations and institutions need common understandings in order to operate effectively.

What kinds of communication are needed for excellence? Six are outlined here: information sharing, feedback, appraisal, problem solving, innovation dialog, and conflict management.

INFORMATION SHARING

In a well-designed system, members freely share with one another whatever information is needed to get the work of the system done.

In hierarchical systems information moves freely both horizontally and vertically. For instance, ABC's executive team uses regularly scheduled meetings to exchange the information they need. However, the length of the meeting is determined by the objectives they want to accomplish. If there is little information to be exchanged, the meeting is deferred. An electronic mail program not only gets essential information to all team members immediately, but also cuts down on the need for meetings. In the best systems, people are reinforced for sharing essential information. Withholding such information from co-workers is a pet strategy in systems pervaded by a competitive, win-lose climate. Each member is out for himself or herself, and withholding information—if it leads to personal gain—is reinforced.

Gilbert (1978), as we have seen, stresses the importance of clear goals. He is also high on relevant, clear, accurate, and timely data.[1]

> Improved information has more potential than anything else I can think of for creating more competence in the day-to-day management of performance. But, as the behavior engineering model. . . points out, we can improve information in two general ways:
>
> 1. We can improve the clarity, relevance, and timeliness of the data designed to inform people.
>
> 2. We can improve people's ability to use the existing data.
>
> Training is an attempt to create a permanent change in people's repertories—most often, in their ability to process difficult data. As an alternative, we can work on the data—to try to make them simpler and clearer, thus easier to understand without extensive training. . . .
> In my experience, one strategem tends to pay off more often—and pay off dramatically: to improve the data designed to support performance. (p. 175)

Poor communication is one of the major sources of ineffectiveness and inefficiency in organizations and institutions.

EXAMPLE: A therapist at a VA hospital felt that he was making progress with a marine who had been wounded in the Middle East and had returned in poor physical and psychological shape. The marine's depression was beginning to abate and some meaningful

---

[1]From *Human Competence: Engineering Worthy Performance* (p. 175) by T.F. Gilbert, 1978, New York: McGraw-Hill. Reprinted by permission.

discussions about his future had taken place. However, he missed a therapy session. When contacted by the therapist, he came, but he seemed rather listless and uncommunicative. After some investigation, the therapist discovered two things. First, the marine's younger brother had been shot and wounded in a tavern. Second, he had been told that he needed surgery. Neither the social service department nor the medical department had communicated this information to the therapist so that he could help the marine manage the crisis.

The therapist did not receive the information he needed in order to carry out his part of the therapeutic program.

In many companies the question is: How do we turn data into information and information into power by getting it into the right hands?

EXAMPLE: A company located in the Northwest was struggling desperately to turn itself around. It had gone through the usual cost-cutting exercises and was now lean, but there were still problems. In many ways the left hand did not know what the right hand was doing. Sales and marketing were doing a pretty good job in landing new projects, but they failed miserably in communicating customer needs to research and development and to manufacturing. For instance, the right products were shipped to customers but in the wrong kind of packaging. This caused all sorts of trouble on the customer's assembly line. The solution was simple. The three units met and drew up a comprehensive form or check list to be used by sales and marketing. This enabled their people to get the right information in the first place. The filled-out form was sent immediately via electronic mail to the other two departments. Ambiguities were immediately clarified and customers began getting what they wanted.

This company's original complaint was a lack of teamwork. However, the real problem was that they were sloppy in *most* of their information-sharing procedures.

Information Technology

Computers, of course, allow for a whole new world of information gathering, analysis, and sharing. Various names are given to departments that provide the technology and processes for managing information: information technology, information services, information-management systems, management-information systems. Even small firms, institutions, and agencies can benefit enormously from the power of the personal computer. Electronic mail systems stimulate communication among organizational units and team members. The information-management officer takes his or her place on the executive team as a key contributor to strategy (Keefe, 1987). Expert information acquisition and flow are providing a competitive edge for many companies.

However, computer technology has also brought a welter of problems. In many cases technology outpaces the organization's overall conception of and policies for information use. There are endless fights over precisely which technology to use and who is to have access to what kind of information. The technology people are accused of not understanding the information needs of the system; managers are accused of being "techno-peasants" (Naisbitt & Aburdene, 1985). Many people, including senior managers, resist the new systems. Middle managers, with some justification, feel that they may be replaced by computers. And, of course, there is the perennial "garbage in, garbage out" problem. Despite these problems, computer literacy will become more and more part of the person specification package in hiring and promoting, and computerized information-management systems are the order of the day.

FEEDBACK

In a well-designed system the members receive feedback first of all from the work itself. This is possible, of course, only if work outcomes, work programs, and other expectations are clear. Then, as needed, members receive from others both confirmatory feedback when things are going well and timely corrective feedback when they are not. All sources of feedback—from peers, supervisors, and customers—are open and operative. Giving effective feedback is an improbable event in many systems. Some people don't seem to realize how important it is; others don't know how to give it or are reluctant to do so.

Lack of ongoing feedback can be a problem at any level with a company or institution. John Sculley (1987), the CEO of Apple Computer, describes the decline of the Macintosh division and the inability of Steve Jobs, Apple's founder, to manage it. Finally, when Sculley tells him that he intends to remove him from his role as executive vice president in charge of the Mac division, Jobs appears "stunned." What happened here? Was it too difficult to give a founder hard messages early on? Did Sculley make the mistake of saving up the hardest messages and delivering them as a judgment? For whatever reason, ongoing feedback was either not given or it was not heard.

> EXAMPLE: ABC Airways, in restructuring itself from top to bottom, realizes that a culture of feedback is absolutely necessary. In many of its organizational units there is a culture of nonfeedback. Hard messages have been withheld for years. Therefore, the CEO feels that he must make a point of announcing this new direction publicly. He insists on getting feedback himself, and he models by providing it for those who report to him. The name of the performance planning and appraisal system is changed to the performance planning, feedback, and appraisal system.

Announcing a culture of feedback is meaningless unless it is driven down into the guts of the system. This may mean training people in the art of giving feedback. Researchers have dubbed the reluctance that all of us feel to be the bearer of bad news the "MUM effect" (Rosen & Tesser, 1970, 1971; Tesser & Rosen, 1972; Tesser, Rosen, & Batchelor 1972; Tesser, Rosen, & Tesser, 1971). They discovered that people tend not to give corrective feedback even when the recipient is explicity open to it. That is, while potential givers of corrective feedback let themselves think that they are being sensitive to the feelings of others, it is often their own feelings with which they are concerned. Since giving feedback is not always a joy in and of itself, giving feedback consistently needs to be rewarded in the system.

Technology and Feedback. Mrs. Fields' Cookies has a computer-based management system that enables Debbi Fields to keep track of every store. The system is designed to free store managers from the burden of administrative detail. They simply set targets for each store and, according to *Financial Weekly* ("Sugar and Spice," 1987):

> [The system] schedules practically every routine activity that must be done. These targets allow the company to operate on a "management by exception" basis. The computer tells the workers in the store if they are not meeting their targets as well as how many cookies they must put in the oven at a particular time to meet a target. (p. 34)

Debbi Fields says that the system provides instant feedback and frees store managers to help, support, and nurture people. Obviously, this would have to be checked out with the people who work in the stores.

Without good ongoing feedback, appraisals turn into judgments. For instance, a man who was recently fired asked why he was being fired. He was told that "the bottom line has not been right for the last year and a half." This was the first time he heard of management's displeasure. If frequent feedback from co-workers and supervisors is added to self-feedback, then ongoing evaluation becomes a reality that eliminates the need for traumatic end-of-the-project or end-of-the-year evaluation.

APPRAISAL

Appraisal refers to the process through which the overall performance of the employee takes place. Appraisal meetings may take place at the end of a project, semiannually, or annually. As important as appraisal is, it works only if (a) direction, objectives, and expectations are clear to both supervisor and worker in the first place and (b) there has been sufficient *ongoing* feedback to help the worker correct mistakes and stay on track. I believe that the main reason that managers hate appraisal meetings is that they have failed to clarify expectations and provide ongoing feedback. This places too much of a burden on appraisal. The result is that devastating messages are delivered only at appraisal time or the appraisal system becomes a joke.

EXAMPLE: Managers in a large service organization complained to a consultant about the performance-appraisal system. They said that they could not say anything negative in the written report for a variety of reasons. One of the principal reasons was the fact that if they did, they could not get any other unit in the organization to take the marginal worker. Appraisal meetings tended to be *pro forma* events with which neither supervisors nor staff members felt satisfied. In this organization, little had been done to institute realistic objective setting and ongoing feedback. This, coupled with an unannounced policy of lifetime employment, made an effective appraisal system impossible and created a cadre of the "living dead" who floated around the organization.

The "living dead" can be found in many organizations, even ones considered excellent in many other ways. Some of the common problems associated with the performance-appraisal meeting are as follows:

- A *pro forma* appraisal with little meaning for the individual or the organization.
- Failure to hold the appraisal meeting.
- Failure of the subordinate to be active in the appraisal process.
- Failure to deal with strengths as well as weaknesses.
- Failure to spell out the implications of the appraisal.
- Failure to set objectives for the next time period.
- Dealing poorly with the conflict around transferring or terminating an employee.
- Dealing poorly with the conflict around nonpromotion.

In the best organizations and institutions, appraisal meetings are not deadly events but further opportunities for productivity- and QWL-oriented communication. Ideally, the appraisal meeting completes the feedback process and leads into a new round of performance planning.

PROBLEM SOLVING

When things go wrong in many companies and institutions, a great deal of effort is made to discover which department or which person to blame. A culture of blaming rather than a culture of problem solving, especially preventive problem solving, is in place.

EXAMPLE: As indicated earlier, it takes a great deal of cooperation among departments to get an airplane away from the gate on time. In ABC there had been a history of blaming the other guy. In its effort to become a premier airline, ABC instituted regular meetings among all units contributing to the departure of airplanes. Their task: preventive problem solving.

Schein (1985) refers to the need in organizations for "mechanisms for correction." A culture of interpersonal and interunit problem solving is one of those mechanisms.

A culture of problem solving does not evolve on its own; it needs to be nurtured. In fact, systematic problem solving is a relatively improbable event. As Miller, Galanter, and Pribam (1960) put it:

> In ordinary affairs we usually muddle ahead, doing what is habitual and customary, being slightly puzzled when it sometimes fails to give the intended outcome, but not stopping to worry much about the failures because there are still too many other things still to do.... An ordinary person almost never approaches a problem systematically and exhaustively unless he or she has been specifically educated to do so. (pp. 171, 174)

Even though this research was published in 1960, I have found no convincing evidence to demonstrate that things are different today. People need to be trained to be effective problem solvers. Such training does not take place in the school system. Since problem solving is considered a key life skill, it is amazing that society leaves acquiring this skill to chance.

Robson (1986) suggests that group problem solving might help:[2]

> It is surprising that most people and organizations tend not to use any form of problem-solving structure or organized methodology for exploiting opportunities. As a result, we tend...to tackle problems by "bumbling through" using a mixture of intuition and experience.... An alternative is to work in groups, but as far as working in groups is concerned, many organizations shy away from it because it is rather more dangerous.... Maybe there is an intuitive worry about losing control or getting the "wrong" answer (defined as someone else's rather than mine!). (pp. 134-135)

The problem here is not just the willingness of managers to trust the collective wisdom of the group. Rather group problem solving is even more difficult than individual problem solving. Quality circles work, in part, because their members are trained in group problem-solving skills (Fox, 1987).

A few years ago I asked an executive at one of the Bell companies what his major complaint about his managers was. He said, instantly, "They're lousy problem solvers." He said that they used a hunt-and-peck problem-solving model. When something went wrong,

---

[2]From *Journey to Excellence* (pp. 134-135) by M. Robson, 1986, Chichester (United Kingdom): John Wiley. Copyright 1986 by John Wiley. Reprinted with permission.

they tried to fix it one way, and when that did not work, they tried a range of solutions until one worked. Obviously, more efficient problem-solving models exist (Egan, 1986, 1988), but people need to be trained in them if they are to move beyond the hunt-and-peck method.

INNOVATION DIALOG

Problem solving among units or among team members within units, even preventive problem solving, is not enough because the focus is still problems, rather than opportunity and innovation. Current and projected turbulent environments call for creativity and innovation at every level within a company or institution. Naisbitt and Aburdene (1985, p. 136) state that in an "information-rich, decentralized, global society, creativity will be increasingly valued in business. Creativity is the corporation's competitive edge. It is the special talent that discovers the right market niche."

Peters and Waterman (1982) describe an innovation-dialog system instituted by Dana Corporation:[3]

> The major pressure at Dana—and it's a very real one. . .is peer pressure. Dana's effort to foster it is capped by Hell Week. Twice a year about a hundred managers get together for five days to swap results and productivity improvement stories. . . . McPherson [the CEO] encouraged the process. . . . He says, "You can always fool the boss. I did. But you can't hide from your peers. They know what's really going on." (p. 252)

It goes without saying that innovation dialogs can take place more frequently than twice a year.

EXAMPLE: The director of marketing for ABC asked his managers and supervisors to have people who work in their units set aside one hour per week in which the sole focus would be, "How can we carry out our business more innovatively and productively?" This could be

---

[3]Excerpt from *In Search of Excellence: Lessons from America's Best-Run Companies* by Thomas J. Peters & Robert H. Waterman, Jr. Copyright © 1982 by Thomas J. Peters & Robert H. Waterman, Jr. Reprinted by permission of Harper & Row, Publishers, Inc.

done on one's own, in small groups, and both ways. Every second week the units would meet to share in a brainstorming way (that is, no criticism, but only clarification and piggybacking) all the ideas generated. The very fact that an hour per week was set aside for innovative thinking helped establish a culture which said, "Innovative ideas are welcome here."

This approach moves closer to establishing innovative thinking as part of the company culture. Robinson (see "Creativity for the Masses," 1987, pp. 12, 15) suggests that organizations can help "grow" creativity and innovation in their employees through such methods as "creativity circles." The purpose of these volunteer groups is to come up with creative ideas and solutions to business problems. She even suggests that the organization should designate an overall creativity coordinator who reports directly to top management. Creativity circles can contribute significantly to QWL. According to Robinson, creativity circles improve morale. Employees who feel they are growing, developing, and learning new skills offer their companies much more than those who are just waiting for their next paycheck. The mental stimulation of creativity training—and creative problem solving— can be a real upper.

This is one approach. Innovation dialog can become part of the system's culture in a whole range of ways. In 1984 the Paul Revere Insurance Companies made an explicit move to establish innovation as a central part of their culture (Townsend, 1986). In 1984 they established a "quality has value" process that focused on quality *teams* in which everyone in the corporation participated, thus moving beyond the more traditional volunteer-oriented quality circle. The purpose of the teams was to promote both quality in fact and quality in perception. However, while quality was certainly a central focus, the process and the results generated had just as much to do with system-wide problem solving and innovation:

> The results are spectacular, a quantum leap forward from other [quality-promotion] methods currently used. In 1984, the first year of Quality Has Value, combining value analysis recommendations and the use of over 4,110 ideas contributed by 1,200 employees, the company was able to realize a saving of over $8.5 million on an annualized basis. The same process has had even more dramatic results in 1985. (p. xv)

Paul Revere seems to have established a culture of creativity and innovation and not just a more traditional quality program.

CONFLICT MANAGEMENT

One of the most important types of communication in organizations, institutions, and communities centers around the management of conflict (see Fisher & Ury, 1981; Robert, 1982; Thomas, 1976; Walton, 1987). Conflict is one of those realities that is so built into the warp and woof of being human that, while needing little definition, it can demand a great deal of attention. Thomas and Schmidt (1976) found that middle managers spent over 25 per cent of their time managing some sort of conflict. Conflict is a state in which the needs, wants, concerns, or interests of two or more parties seem to be incompatible. Thomas (1976, p. 891) defines conflict as "the process which begins when one party perceives that the other has frustrated, or is about to frustrate, some concern of his or hers."

While conflict, as one form of crisis, is instinctively associated with the negative connotations of that term, that is, disturbed relationships and emotional turmoil, it can also be seen as an opportunity. The word *crisis* comes from a Greek word meaning to divide or to decide. Conflict as a form of crisis is a time for deciding, it is a choice point. Ideally it is a time to review available options and to make choices that lead to constructive outcomes. That is, conflict is not just inevitable, it is also potentially useful. Energy need not be poured into preventing it since avoiding conflict is tantamount to avoiding an opportunity for growth.

A Negotiation Model

Fisher and Ury (1981) have some extremely useful suggestions for negotiating win-win solutions to conflict. These are outlined below, using a case of a social worker and her supervisor.

• **Interests Versus Positions.** Separate the positions that people take in conflict situations from the interests that underlie these positions. A social worker in conflict with her supervisor about overtime needs to examine both her interests and the interests of the agency. A "you must" position on the part of the supervisor and an "I won't" position on the part of the social worker will probably only escalate the conflict.

• **Issues Versus Personality Disputes.** The issues must be separated from the personal problems the conflicting parties have with one another. The interpersonal problems need to be addressed separately from, in this case, work-related issues. If the social worker's supervisor hints that their relationship depends on her adopting his position on overtime, she must insist that the issue being discussed is not the relationship, but fairness in work practices.

• **The Exploration of Mutual Interests.** Headway can be made if both parties back away from their positions and explore the interest underlying these positions in a search for *mutual* interests. In this case, both the social worker and her supervisor are interested in the welfare of clients. Both are also interested in fostering quality of work life.

• **Solutions Based on Mutual Interests.** Negotiating on the basis of positions rather than interests leads either to the escalation of the conflict or to solutions that satisfy no one. On the other hand, once interests are explored and mutual interests identified, win-win solutions can be pursued. For instance, if some of the social worker's overtime can be considered compensatory time, which can be used later when the agency has a slack period, then the interests of both the social worker and the agency (as represented by the supervisor) can be met. Problem solving takes the place of positional bargaining.

The Fisher and Ury model has been used successfully in a wide range of conflict situations, from political and cultural impasses in the Middle East to renegotiating the lease for an apartment.

I used a form of this model with a manufacturing firm mentioned earlier. First, an "organizational mirror" exercise was used to help conflicting parties get the issues on the table. In this exercise, manufacturing was asked to guess what marketing's "bitch list" about them would be and, of course, marketing was asked to engage in the same process. When the lists were shared, each was amazed at how perceptive the other was. And since each unit was allowed to "get itself" instead of being got or confronted by the other, a hostile climate was avoided. Then key issues to be negotiated were chosen and negotiating teams from each unit, after being coached in the Fisher and Ury model, were asked to use it. Afterward, people from these two units said that they had never engaged in such constructive dialog before and wondered why they had stuck so steadfastly to their usual adversarial approaches.

Outcomes

A conflict can be said to be resolved when the parties in question are fully satisfied with an outcome. This means that there is either no residual frustration or at least not enough to precipitate future episodes. However, conflict, like most human problems, is not solved or resolved, but managed. The fact that today's frustration is managed more or less is no guarantee that tomorrow will not spawn its own. When two parties emerge from a conflict, the bottom-line questions deal with productivity and quality of life:

- Did they come up with a decision that they both can live with, at least for now?

- Does this decision in some way favor, or at least not stand in the way of, the productivity of the system?

- Is the relationship between the two parties still intact and workable?

- Does the decision help improve, or at least not stand in the way of, the quality of life of other members?

- Does the quality of the decision merit its financial and psychological costs? If not, what has been learned that can contribute to making conflict management in this system more cost effective in the future?

- Has this conflict situation helped the parties reflect on and clarify personal values, system values, and the interaction between the two?

Here are some questions about both interunit and interpersonal communication within units.

Interunit Communication

- To what degree do we establish terms of reference for our interactions with other relevant organizational units?
- How well does this unit share information needed for productivity with other units in the organization?
- To what degree do we get the information we need from other units?
- To what degree do we give feedback to and get feedback from other units with respect to products or services in order to increase productivity?
- In what ways do we engage constructively with other units in the appraisal of one another's performance?
- How well do we engage in collaborative problem solving with other units?
- To what degree do we have innovation-focused dialogs with other units?
- How effectively do we work through conflicts with other units in the system?

Interpersonal Communication

- How well do we see one another in this unit as internal customers?
- How effectively do we share information with one another in this unit?
- How open are we to giving feedback to and receiving feedback from one another?
- How realistic are our appraisals of one another in this unit?
- What is the quality of collaborative problem solving in this unit?
- To what degree do we engage in innovation dialogs in this unit?
- How effectively do we handle conflicts with one another in this unit?

15

The Reward System: Keeping Motivation High

B. F. Skinner (1953) started a revolution (and a controversy) by systematically developing the principles underlying behavior and its modification. Indeed, the term *behavior modification* raises hackles even today for those who do not distinguish it from *brainwashing*. Yet, a great deal of research over the last thirty years has culminated in sophisticated compilations of these principles and their application to everyday behavior, social learning, personality development, abnormal behavior, self-management, and, of course to the behavior of people in organizations (see Luthans & Kreitner, 1975; Miller, 1978). These principles are sometimes called principles of learning because they describe the ways in which people learn (and unlearn) to do things in both self-enhancing (and organization-enhancing) and self-limiting (and organization-limiting) ways. Indeed, Skinner's work helped change the focus from the more mysterious terms *motivation* to the more understandable and manageable terms *incentives* and *rewards*.

MOTIVATION:
ANTECEDENTS AND CONSEQUENCES

There have been endless treatises and debates about motivation, that is, people's willingness to engage in work leading to accomplishments. Herzberg (1987) makes a critical distinction between motivation and movement:[1]

---

[1]Reprinted by permission of the *Harvard Business Review*. An excerpt from "One More Time: How Do You Motivate Employees?" by Frederick Herzberg (January-February 1968). Copyright © 1968 by the President and Fellows of Harvard College; all rights reserved.

Movement is a function of fear of punishment or failure to get *extrinsic* rewards. . . . Motivation is a function of growth [creativity, productivity] from getting *intrinsic* rewards out of interesting and challenging work. While the immediate behavioral results from movement and motivation appear alike [accomplishments, outputs, work done], their dynamics, which produce vastly different long-term consequences, are different. Movement requires constant reinforcement [or supervisory control] and stresses short-term results. To get a reaction, management must constantly enhance the extrinsic rewards for movement. If I get a bonus of $1,000 one year and $500 the next, I am getting extra [extrinsic] rewards both years, but psychologically I have taken a $500 salary cut. Motivation is based on growth needs. It is an internal engine, and its benefits show up over a long period of time [emphasis added]. (p. 118)

Motivation is a function of incentives and rewards. There is a high degree of motivation in an organization—the incentive/reward system is working—if people consistently get the work done efficiently (productivity) with a reasonable degree of sastisfaction (quality of work life).

The ABCs of Motivation

A simple ABC (antecedents, behaviors, consequences) model illustrated in Figure 15-1 is useful in understanding motivation. The dotted line indicates that in some way the consequences come back to enhance (or haunt) our behavior. Consider the behavior of a supervisor in the engineering maintenance department of ABC Airways.

From the supervisor's point of view, noticing the error is an *antecedent* that acts as a stimulus to the *behavior* of giving feedback. Since the *consequence* of giving feedback is experienced as rewarding, the supervisor continues to give feedback in the same way.

Consider another example in Figure 15-2.

ABC employees experience the consequence as rewarding and make further efforts to maintain and even increase productivity. On the other hand, the world is filled with cases in which antecedents (unappealing incentives) and consequences (ineffective rewards, punishing work conditions) conspire to break the system down.

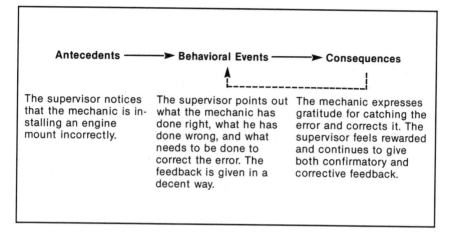

Figure 15-1. Feedback on Performance

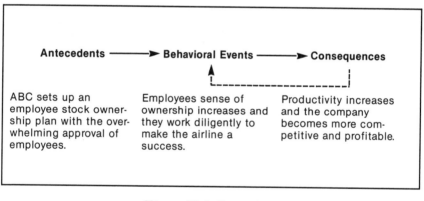

Figure 15-2. Incentives

In summary, motivation (as opposed to movement) can best be seen in terms of antecedents called incentives and consequences called rewards rather than as a "black box" buried within each individual which needs to be manipulated or fixed. As Gilbert (1978) notes, when a manager says that a worker does not have any motivation, he or she really means that the incentive/reward system is poor. Odds are that this is the fault of the manager or the system rather than of the worker.

INCENTIVES:
CRITICAL SYSTEM ANTECEDENTS

Perhaps incentives constitute the most critical set of antecedents for system functioning. An incentive is a kind of promise that performance will be rewarded (and that nonperformance will not be rewarded). In some organizations there is a great deal of talk about motivation but too little talk about incentives (see Gilbert, 1978, pp. 83-97, 309-316). While motivation is difficult to pin down, incentives are manageable. In effective systems both *extrinsic* incentives such as decent wages and a bonus system and *intrinsic* incentives such as work autonomy or the desire to do a good job are operative. Gilbert (1978) states:[2]

> The two causes of poor performance most commonly espoused are motives ("they don't care") and capacity ("they're too dumb.") But these are ususally the last two places one should look for causes of incompetence, simply because they rarely are the substantial problem. . . . Except for a few strange individuals, people generally care a great deal about how they perform on the job, or in school. . . . Improvements in training can do wonders for most people we consider slow-witted; better incentives can usually obliterate all evidence of defective motivation. (p. 89)

When managers say that "the people who work here are not motivated," they often do so because it is much more difficult to say, "I have not been very inventive in discovering, through collaboration with the people who report to me, the kinds of incentives that made sense to them."

In discussing incentives, Gilbert (1978) lays down six principles for creating *incompetence* in an organization:[3]

- Make sure that poor performers get paid as well as good ones.
- See that good performance gets punished in some way.

---

[2]From *Human Competence: Engineering Worthy Performance* (p. 89) by T.F. Gilbert, 1978, New York: McGraw-Hill. Reprinted by permission.

[3]Ibid., p. 87.

- Design the job so that it has no future.
- Avoid arranging working conditions that employees would find more pleasant.
- Give pep talks rather than incentives to promote performance in punishing situations. (p. 87)

Herzberg (1987) suggests that the best kinds of incentives (he calls them "motivators") are intrinsic to getting the work done—direct feedback from the work itself, control over resources, self-scheduling, personal accountability, authority to get things done, recognition, learning from both internal and external clients, and the like. Indeed, unless workers get most of their satisfaction, in one way or another, from the work itself and producing results, the system is in trouble.

Many people find satisfaction in simply knowing that they are doing a job competently and that they are fulfilling their part of a contract. This is even true of workers in very humdrum jobs. If jobs can be made less humdrum, all the better, and if certain extrinsic rewards can help take the bite out of a boring job—for instance, the paper work that most managers are subjected to—then they should be used. Even better, get a computerized information-management system that dramatically reduces paper work. In any case, it is a mistake to assume, on the one hand, that no one can experience intrinsic rewards in even grinding jobs (ask coal miners) or, on the other hand, that people do not complain about such jobs because they do not know any better or cannot do anything else.

To suggest that intrinsic reinforcement can be and often is operative even in grinding work is not to romanticize such work. Grinding work can grind up workers both physically and psychologically (Rubin, 1976; Terkel, 1974). Undoubtedly, advances in technology, rearrangement and improvement of working conditions, and a more sensible and liberal use of extrinsic rewards can make a more humane experience. But it is quite possible to exploit a worker's need to do a job competently and his or her desire to fulfill even an unjust contract. Here we come face to face with value issues. O'Toole's (1985) research on "vanguard" companies suggests that the best systems do things because they are right in both a business and moral sense.

REWARDS: BEHAVIOR AS A FUNCTION
OF ITS CONSEQUENCES

A number of important principles relate to the consequences of behavior. The most important is that behavior is a function of its consequences, that is, patterns of behavior are strengthened, maintained, or weakened by events that follow them. For instance, guards in a correctional facility are more likely to consistently pass on information that their superiors need to make staffing decisions if such information sharing is encouraged and praised rather than taken for granted. When people come late for and show apathy during meetings, it is their way of saying that such meetings are experienced as punitive rather than rewarding. Meetings that produce things of value—problem solving, needed information, decisions—are usually not avoided.

Take something as simple as letting people know that they are doing a good job. Everyone knows that corrective feedback (often poorly delivered) is more probable than confirmatory ("that was a good job") feedback. Common sense and research both urge more confirmatory feedback. Why? People experience it as rewarding and a reward is a consequence that tends to strengthen the behavior it follows. And yet managers and supervisors see it as "soft" and fail to use it. Kenneth Lay, the CEO of Enron, the country's largest pipeline company ($7.6 billion in sales in 1986) makes confirmatory feedback part of his managerial style and the overall reward system of the company (Mack, 1987):

> Ken gives subordinates lots of authority, pay, and attention. He put the stock he bought from Jacobs and Leucadia into an ESOP [employee stock ownership plan], then traveled the country to tell employees that they owned 20% of Enron's common. "The loyalty to Ken," says Mick Seidl, "is a function of his paying attention to people and letting them be entrepreneurial." "You can imagine," adds Jim Rogers, "how excited young people four or five levels down in the organization get when the chairman of the board calls to tell them, 'You're doing great.' (p. 62)

Lay's "softness" in such areas as employee ownership, autonomy, and recognition has paid off in loyalty and hard profits.

Customizing Incentives and Rewards

In an effectively functioning system, the incentives are clear and abundant and the rewards they imply are conferred as promised. However, since different people are motivated by different incentives, it is up to each company or institution to get its own package of incentives and rewards right. No single formula applies to everyone. Managers and supervisors in each organizational unit have to ask, "Do we have our package of incentives and rewards right?" For instance, a number of organizations are currently letting workers choose the benefits they want. They set a dollar figure for benefits and then give each worker a menu from which he or she can choose. Younger workers might choose one package; older workers, another. Such a system provides autonomy and respects the principle, "What is an incentive for Jane might not be an incentive for John."

PUNISHMENT

I was in a meeting in which an airport manager was talking about problems with baggage handlers and ticket sellers (the real problem turned out to be ineffective supervisors). At one point in the conversation, the director of personnel interjected, "We know how to punish when we have to." I glanced over at him and immediately knew that he was right. What about punishment? Often enough in life it is one of the consequences of behavior that is seen as unacceptable. There are two kinds of punishment, both involving some unpleasant consequence:

1. A person's behavior leads to an unpleasant consequence: An ABC flight attendant is caught cheating in his duty-free accounts and is fired.

2. A person's behavior leads to the loss of something desired. An ABC maintenance supervisor is frequently late and takes too many breaks. She fails to get the promotion she expected.

Punishment does work, at least in the short run; that is, it does tend to lessen unwanted behavior. For instance, the director of the young-professionals program at ABC, after telling an intern that he will suspend her for two weeks if she arrives late again or misses another day of work, actually does so when she misses a day. The result is that she no longer comes late nor misses work. Although punishment does tend to make unwanted behavior less probable, it often does so at a price, that is, there are often some unwanted side effects:

- The effect of punishment is often temporary.
- It leads to no new learning.
- Punished people often find devious ways of avoiding the punishment.
- It can cause emotional disruption, such as the loss of face or self-esteem. Or the punished person sees the punisher as bad and learns to fear and/or dislike the person.
- It can lead to the suppression of *wanted* behavior. While punishment might inhibit unwanted behavior, it can also in-hibit desirable behavior that is related to the punished behavior. Consider the following example.

EXAMPLE: When the technology and design team of an electronics firm suggested a new product to senior management, they were told to design what they were told to design. Of course, they felt punished. Later, when given a product to design, they soon learned that it would cost too much and therefore not be very marketable. They said nothing. Senior management discovered the same thing—but some hundreds of thousands of dollars later.

This is not to suggest that punishment can or even should be eliminated from human life. This is impossible. However, too many of us give into punishing others because of the emotional payoff it has (venting) and its short-term effects. On balance, minimizing punishment in companies and institutions is good business.

Reducing the Need for Punishment Through Effective Manage-ment. Good management reduces the need for rules and discipline and therefore reduces the amount of punishment in a system. Ground rules and disciplinary procedures set the limits within which people operate, but they do not provide incentives for doing well. If rules, disciplinary procedures, and punishment for violations are central, then the system is poorly managed. After all, disciplinary policies set the limits on how *poor* performance can be and shall be tolerated. Good management—which includes the intelligent use of incentives and rewards, especially the intrinsic rewards of experiencing oneself as competent and doing well, confirmatory and corrective feedback, and the effective use of system design—is aimed at helping workers bring performance above absolute minimums so that disciplinary actions need not be used. Enforcing rules in order to get minimally acceptable performance on the part of the members of a system is poor management. Stimulating and reinforcing good performance is much more interesting and important, for it minimizes the need to be an enforcer (see Brethower, 1972).

AVOIDANCE BEHAVIOR

Avoidance behavior calls for special attention because it insidiously affects our participation in all the systems of our lives and because it is highly resistant to extinction. It is my conviction that avoidance behavior is central to the "psychopathology of the average" and underlies the failed potential of both individuals and human systems. Consider the following example.

EXAMPLE: ABC's VP of operations had been talked into adding a level called flight supervisors to the cabin-crew system by the director of cabin crew services. These supervisors were supposed to provide coaching, counseling, and feedback to flight attendants on the ground. The supervisory position was part-time; they flew the rest of the time. The system did not work. Since the flight supervisors were not good at coaching and counseling, they began to do administrative things, which were seen as useless by the flight attendants. The flight supervisors were also resented because they "didn't pull their weight" by flying enough. The VP told the director to phase out the system. The latter, however, avoided doing anything about it because of the upheaval it would cause. The VP said nothing. The system persisted and caused even more unrest.

The problem with avoidance behavior is that it is immediately rewarded. The director of cabin crew services, by putting off the VP's directive, was rewarded by not having to face the upheaval; that is, there was the immediate relief of not having to face an unpleasant situation. This "reward" raises the probability that this kind of avoidance behavior will be repeated in the future. The fact that the VP said nothing reinforced the avoidance. Avoidance, like punishment, eliminates new learning. And once a pattern of avoidance becomes habitual, then it becomes even more impervious to management. It goes underground and is not even recognized any longer as avoidance behavior.

Effectively functioning systems are not immune to avoidance behavior, but they have a realization that avoidance is both common, insidious, and difficult to deal with. The point is that avoidance behavior is one of the primary sources of individual- and system-limiting arationality. Without being pessimistic, wise managers, administrators, and consultants take avoidance behavior as a given and help their organizations and institutions deal with its most debilitating forms. For instance, they build an assessment of avoidance behaviors into their periodic reviews. One of the questions that is always on the agenda is: "What are we currently avoiding and what negative impact is this avoidance having on the system?" Such systems are eager for new learning that creates more options for the system, its members, and the people it serves. In effectively functioning systems, avoidance of the legitimate tasks of the system and failure are not rewarded. Employees are not rewarded for not working, students for not learning, supervisors for not giving feedback, and so forth.

Here are some questions about incentives and rewards:

- To what degree is getting the work of the system done the primary reward in this system?
- To what degree are there incentives in all units to accomplish goals?
- What kind of disincentives interfere with our work?
- To what degree are incentives followed by meaningful rewards? What promises are made but not kept?
- To what extent do we have the right mix of incentives and rewards for our work force?
- How effectively do individuals establish meaningful reward systems for themselves?
- To what degree is the system managed so as to avoid punishment?
- To what degree is there a "culture of avoidance" in the system?
- How are avoiders treated?

16

Individual Performance Plans

The planning process, as we have seen, is a way of driving the strategy down into the guts of the organization. The individual performance plan, the third kind of planning considered here, is the individual counterpart of unit performance planning. Ideally, each person in the organization draws up his or her own individual plan in consultation with a manager or supervisor. The plan is an opportunity for each individual to review all of the issues related to the organizational dimensions of the model—for instance, his or her roles together with the responsibilities they involve—in order to set priorities and objectives that contribute in substantive ways to the fulfillment of the unit performance plan. The purpose of the individual performance plan is to help each person in the unit answer two questions:

1. What are the things that I am expected to do in order to see to it that the unit performance plan is executed?

2. Against the background of all the tasks that constitute my role in the unit, what are my priorities this period (usually a year)?

For instance, the manager of the management development unit of ABC Airways, Karen, after completing her unit performance plan, outlines her own priorities, that is, those things that she especially wants to accomplish because of their contribution to the unit performance plan and the overall ABC strategy. Since many new people will be in both managerial and supervisory positions, courses need to be mounted to give them some basic skills and, perhaps even more important, socialize them into the managerial culture that fits the overall ABC strategy. Another priority is staffing her unit. She needs to hire two new trainers and bring them up to speed in the unit as quickly as possible. A third priority is to establish working relationships with other training units in the airline, including the other units in the corporate training department and cabin-crew training. She believes that a common philosophy must permeate all forms of training, since training is a form of socialization.

The individual plan also needs to outline what kinds of training and development the person needs to continue to function effectively in his or her role or to move to another role. For instance, Karen needs to be in touch with the state of the art in her area. She needs to visit other companies who have high-quality management training programs; she needs to attend courses or conferences where practical, outcome-oriented programs are offered.

The individual plan also gives individuals an opportunity to review the ways in which current incentives and rewards are functioning in their work lives. For instance, a manager might be doing quite well in his or her current position but feel the need for a change. Karen currently has no problems with either incentives or rewards. She finds ABC with its new mission and strategy an exciting place to work. She is paid reasonably well, but gets most of her satisfaction from the work she is doing. She has been given a reasonable budget, the freedom to find out what pragmatic kinds of management training might make sense in this very pragmatic airline, the autonomy she needs to develop management programs, and access to other managers.

The steps in formulating the individual performance plan are similar to the steps in formulating the unit performance plan.

Step 1: Establish Essential Linkages.

It is essential to link the individual plan to the overall goals and priorities of the unit, just as the unit plan—in this case, the plan of the training unit—needs to be linked to the overall mission and strategy of the airline. The unit plan and priorities constitute one of the data bases for individual plans.

Step 2: List All Personal-Performance Areas.

Karen needs to list all the tasks for which she personally is responsible. Here is a partial list:

- Drawing up and managing the budget of the unit.
- Assessing the training needs of managers.
- Reviewing state-of-the-art management development programs.
- Designing management-training programs for clients.
- Publishing a management-development program guide.
- Setting up a course-registration system.
- Setting up a system to track manager participation.
- Seeing to the development needs of current training staff.
- Hiring and training new staff.
- Developing a common training philosophy with other units involved in training.
- Developing follow-up programs to help managers who have been trained to transfer what they have learned to their units.
- Coaching and counseling her own staff.
- Participating in the reformulation of the mission and strategy of the human resources department of which the management development unit is a part.
- Participating in several HRD task forces.
- Hiring and training course assistants to handle the production of course materials, audiovisual equipment, course registration, and other administrative details.
- Writing some articles on new approaches to management development.
- Providing internal consultancy services for managers who ask.

These and other responsibilities constitute the second data base on which Karen's individual performance plan will be based.

Step 3: Identify Key Personal-Performance Areas.

Key personal-performance areas are those that deserve priority attention on Karen's part during the coming year if she is to promote the strategy (unit performance plan) of the management development unit. What are to be her key result areas, that is, areas in need of special attention because of the strategy of the airline, the strategy of the human resources department, and the strategy of the management development unit? No more than four or five areas should be designated as key. If everything has priority, then nothing has priority. Karen chooses four areas for special attention:

• **Reviewing state-of-the-art programs in basic managerial skills.** The airline right now does not need frills. Managers need to be grounded in a common philosophy and basic skills. Karen realizes that a lot of nonsense has been written about management and that the world is filled with half-baked programs. Too much is at stake. ABC needs the best programs and needs them as soon as possible.

• **Taking the role as team leader in designing the ABC program in basic managerial skills.** This program will be set up for anyone newly appointed to a managerial role and for those who have been managers for less than a year. Karen wants the other members of her team to assist her in this task so that the program produced will be owned by all.

• **Hiring two new trainers and setting up a probation program for one of her staff who is performing poorly.** Trainers in the program have to be credible. Training managers who have been chosen because they are good in some professional or technical area and who do not see management as a science or art in its own right is not an easy task at best. Karen cannot afford second-rate trainers.

• **Participating in the reformulation of the mission and strategy of the human resources department.** The viability of the management development unit depends on the viability of the HR department. The new director wants to change the focus of HR from the delivery of traditional personnel services to one of internal consultancy on managerial and organizational issues. Karen is a firm believer in this new direction but realizes that it will not happen without a great deal of work.

Step 4: Set Priority Individual Objectives in Each Key Performance Area.

When key personal-performance areas have been selected, one to three major performance objectives should be set in each area. These are the actual outcomes, the critical things that will be accomplished in each key area. For instance, with respect to the key personal-performance area "reviewing state-of-the-art programs in basic managerial skills," Karen sets the following objectives:

• Within two months four major books on management-development and management-training programs will have been reviewed from the point of view of providing training objectives and programs;

• Within four months, she will have attended four conferences or courses on management training and will have culled from them models, objectives, and training strategies that seem to fit ABC needs. One of the best ways of choosing training modules, she believes, is to experience them herself.

• Within four months she will have visited four or five companies reputed to have top-quality management development programs and will have collated the best they have to offer in terms of management-training mission, strategy, frameworks, and programs.

The accomplishment of these three objectives will be a substantial contribution to this priority performance area.

Step 5: Develop Personal-Performance Indicators.

Personal-performance indicators are a way of determining whether an objective has been wholly or partially realized by the individual. Performance indicators must be clear enough to enable the individual, fellow staff members, and supervisors to reach a conclusion independently about full or partial fulfillment of each objective. Interim indicators are used throughout the year for ongoing feedback and final indicators are used for year-end review.

Consider Karen's first objective, "Within two months four major books on management-development and management-training programs will have been reviewed from the point of view of providing training objectives and programs." How will she know that this objective has been accomplished?

- **Interim indicators.** She will know that she is making progress if she gets suggestions from people in the field of management development, reads reviews of current offerings, obtains the books, reads them herself, or has others read and summarize some of them.

- **Final indicators.** She will know that she has completed this objective when she has a written report comprised of a number of elements that should be found in the mission of a basic management-development program, a few frameworks that might serve as the basis of the training program (for instance, the Wilson framework described in Chapter 17), a range of possible training objectives, and a range of work programs that will contribute to these objectives. These findings will have been shared with the other members of the team.

An outline of the basic elements of individual performance planning is found in Figure 16-1. However, a caution is in order. This highly rational planning approach is meant to stimulate the members of the staff and help them provide direction for themselves. It should be seen as a flexible framework that can be altered to meet changing individual and unit needs. It is a tool to be tailored to the style of each member and it is not meant to stifle creativity. At best it leaves the staff member and his or her supervisor with an agreed-on document that spells out mutual expectations. But it is a document that may well need renegotiation over the course of the year. Problems arise when organizations forget that individual performance planning is a productivity tool and make it an end in itself. This usually leads to filling out endless forms and other busy work that actually stand in the way of productivity both physically and psychologically. Individual performance planning, reasonably conceived and executed, whether formally or informally, can be a fine integrative management or supervisory tool. However, it can do more harm than good in the hands of the incompetent.

Basis and linkage	Personal performance areas	Key areas	Priority personal objectives in each key area	Outcome indicators for each objective
* Unit plan ──▶○----------------●			1. _____	a ___ b ___ c ___
	○			
* Unit priorities─▶○----------------●			1. _____	a ___ b ___
	○		2. _____	a ___ b ___
	○		3. _____	a ___
	○			
* Job ──▶○----------------● description			1. _____	a ___ b ___
	○			
* Current ──▶○----------------● personal plans			1. _____	a ___ b ___
	○		2. _____	a ___
* Budget ──▶○			3. _____	a ___ b ___ c ___
	○			
* Other ──▶○----------------● planning documents ○			1. _____	a ___ b ___ c ___
			2. _____	a ___

Figure 16-1. Elements of Personal Performance Planning

Figure 16-2 presents in graphic form the principal organizational dimensions. Note that forms of organization at both the unit and the individual level must serve overall and functional business outcomes.

Here are some questions that can be asked about the status of individual performance planning in any organization:

- To what degree are effective performance planning practices in place?

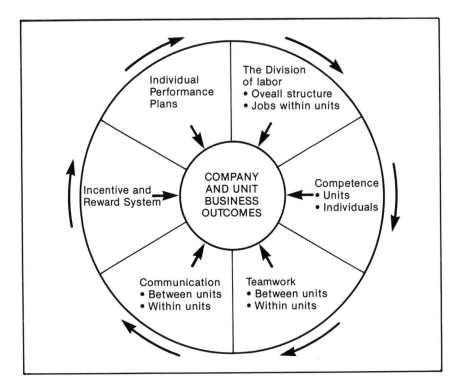

Figure 16-2. Organizational Dimensions Serving Business Outcomes

- To what degree are individual performance plans linked to ongoing feedback and realistic appraisal?
- How collaborative (with managers) is the setting of performance objectives?
- How well do individuals know the priorities of the unit performance plan?
- To what degree is individual performance planning merely *pro forma*? To what degree does it actually drive behavior?
- To what degree are individual plans updated as unit priorities change?
- What might be done to make individual performance planning more effective?

PART III

MANAGEMENT
AND LEADERSHIP

There is a revolution afoot in management and leadership. It has been belatedly discovered that management is part science and part art and that the managerial role demands a specific set of skills. For years people have been promoted to managerial positions without having these skills and have failed to acquire them on the job. The business literature is filled with examples of companies that are in desperate straits because they have been "poorly managed." Many companies and institutions are placing "management development" on their list of priorities. Others, it seems, have yet to be informed of the revolution.

A revolution in thinking about leadership is also afoot. While it has long been known that headship and leadership are not the same, leadership is one of those concepts that means so many things that it means almost nothing. Yet like "excellence" it is one of those worthy terms that each generation needs to clarify for itself. The term is currently being democratized. That is, leadership can be found throughout a company or institution. It is no longer the prerogative of those who are designated to run enterprises or the subunits within them.

Part III deals with working models of both management and leadership and the kinds of skills and behaviors that contribute to system-enhancing outcomes.

17

Effective Management and Leadership

All or much of what has been described in these pages is likely to happen to the degree that a company or institution has effective management and leadership. These two are not the same thing, and both are needed. However, as we shall see, they can both be found in the same person.

EFFECTIVE MANAGEMENT

Managers are managers both of processes and of the people who execute these processes. Both roles are described in the following paragraphs.

Managers of Business and Organizational Processes

The role of the manager as a manager of processes is to see to it that the canons of business and organizational excellence described in these pages are implemented consistently throughout the system. Managers do this by planning, organizing, coordinating, facilitating, and instituting effective controls. For instance, from a business point of view, a marketing manager must see to it that an effective marketing plan, based on overall company strategy, is drawn up and implemented. A plant manager must see to it that quality is built into the company's products. A raw materials manager must establish the kind of relationships with suppliers that assure that suppliers consistently provide high-quality materials at reasonable prices and on time. From an organizational point of view, the head of the intensive care unit must see to it that the members of his or her team work together smoothly and efficiently at providing service for patient survival and improvement. The head of the recruitment department of an investment bank must make certain that highly skilled investors who are compatible with the mission and philosophy of the institution and with the other members of the team are both recruited and socialized into the system. Managers are successful when quality products or services that meet the needs of internal or external customers are delivered expeditiously and cost effectively. In a word, managers are developers and coordinators of all the elements of Model A.

Managers of People

Managers implement the canons of excellence and see to it that the work of the system gets done through *partnerships* with the people they manage. Every good manager knows that without competent, motivated workers he or she is dead in the water. But precisely what does a manager do as a manager of people? Wilson (1983, 1988a, 1988b) provides a simple model of the essential management-of-people practices in what he calls the "management task cycle." The cycle includes six steps: setting goals, developing work programs, facilitating the work of others, providing feedback, making and monitoring whatever adjustments are called for by the feedback, and recognizing and rewarding performance. A few words about each of these steps are in order.

1. **Setting Clear Goals.** Effective managers make sure that workers understand precisely what is expected of them in terms of work outcomes. Even though clarifying outcome expectations is essential for productivity, many mangers do not take the time to do so. As mentioned, this is especially true in the case of human-service outcomes. For instance, the manager of the passenger service department of ABC Airways wants her staff to "treat customers well" but does not spell out what this means in terms of outcomes.

2. **Developing Clear Work Programs.** Effective managers see to it that workers have a clear understanding of the step-by-step work programs that lead to the delivery of business outcomes. They solicit suggestions for designing and improving work programs from those

responsible for carrying them out. And they give workers the autonomy they need to carry them out. For instance, in ABC there are clear and detailed work programs for removing, maintaining, and replacing jet engines. Maintenance crews remember the disaster that occurred when workers in the maintenance department of a competing airline did not follow work-program guidelines. There was engine trouble and the plane crashed.

3. **Facilitating the Execution of Work Programs.** Effective managers do a variety of things to facilitate the work of the people they manage. They make sure that people have the resources they need to get the work done. They provide coaching and counseling. As Karlheinz Kaske, the CEO of Siemens (the German electronics giant) puts it, "You win cooperation by explaining to talented people what you want, then giving them the authority and resources to accomplish it" ("The World's 50 Biggest," 1987, p. 39). ABC trains its managers in coaching and counseling skills so that they can deal with nonperformers more effectively.

4. **Providing Feedback.** Clear work programs leading to clearly defined goals or outcomes enable workers to give themselves feedback. Effective managers consistently complement self-feedback on progress toward goals and quality of outcomes with their own confirmatory or corrective feedback as needed. They do so both formally and informally. For instance, the director of information services at ABC, while delegating the design of a new reservations program to his team, reviewed the team's progress from time to time and provided his input. The director of catering reviewed passenger feedback on ABC's new catering services and provided feedback that helped her team make improvements.

5. **Making and Monitoring Adjustments.** Effective managers make whatever adjustments are needed after receiving feedback from workers (upward communication) or providing corrective feedback to them. For instance, when airline maintenance crews tell their managers they cannot keep everything in the cabin in top-flight condition unless flight attendants pass along passenger complaints as quickly as possible about things such as defective lights or call buttons, then it is up to these managers to talk to their counterparts in cabin crew services to make sure that the two units cooperate. Or, when cabin crew managers tell cabin services supervisors that they

are turning people off by the harsh way in which they give instructions and feedback, the managers need to monitor changes in the supervisors' performance. Follow up may include obtaining training for the supervisors in basic supervisory skills.

6. Rewarding Performance. Effective managers see to it that the system provides adequate incentives to workers and that workers are rewarded for performance. This includes recognizing superior performance in a variety of ways. In ABC, managers are asked to submit names of people who make special contributions, and the names and specific contributions are listed in the airline newspaper.

Figure 17-1 presents a graphic representation of the management-task cycle. It indicates that managers engage in these activities in order to promote business outcomes. Effective managers intervene as often as is necessary at any point in this iterative cycle to make sure that quality products or services are delivered.

EFFECTIVE LEADERSHIP: INNOVATION AND CHANGE

Effective managers keep the system on keel and headed in the direction that has been set. Leaders, on the other hand, do regular things extraordinarily well or make *new* things happen. Leaders see to it that system-enhancing innovations and change take place. Leadership in this sense is not relegated to the top levels of a company or institution. Rather leadership permeates all levels of excellent companies and institutions. The model of leadership offered here is based on the work of Bennis and Nanus (1985) and deals with leadership behaviors and outcomes rather than the qualities of the leader. Since many companies and institutions are currently being battered by competitive environments and massive economic, social, and political change, they must adapt and change or risk mediocrity or even extinction. They need more than effective management; they need leadership. There are five things that leaders do to contribute, not just to the survival and ongoing well-being of the system, but to its quest for improvement. These steps constitute a leadership-task cycle.

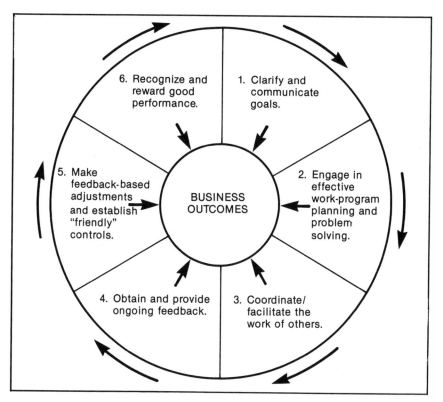

Figure 17-1. Wilson's Management-Task Cycle

1. VISION: Leaders create visions for the company or institution. Leaders, while realistic, are not tied down to the present. In good times they develop visions of an even better future. In bad times they develop visions of survival even when the odds spell doom.

The CEO of ABC Airways has a vision of creating a flexible, cost-effective, customer-centered (especially business customers) international carrier with a straightforward strategy that drives behavior at every level and with a structure that breaks through the bureaucratic organizational procedures that stifle attempts on the part of staff to provide top-quality, innovative service for customers.

2. AGENDAS: Leaders turn their visions into viable agendas. Leaders are not mere visionaries. Their vision and creativity lead to system-enhancing innovation. They translate their visions into challenging but realistic agendas. These agendas become blueprints that set new directions for others in the organization.

The CEO of ABC draws up a blueprint for action. His agenda includes making the structure leaner for greater flexibility, turning the organizational pyramid on its side with middle managers supporting frontline staff in their interactions with customers, giving frontline staff the authority to take risks in servicing customers, making certain international routes or markets are distinct business units with both the authority and responsibility needed to compete with any other airline in that market, acquiring one or two troubled carriers for bargain prices, establishing two new domestic hubs, and entering collaborative relationships with feeder airlines.

3. COMMUNICATION: Leaders arouse enthusiasm and loyalty by the way they communicate their agendas. Leaders, whether personally reserved or outgoing, are good communicators in the sense that they get people to rally around their agendas. They do not try to sell people a bill of goods. Rather their agendas speak for themselves; they are appealing because they are both challenging and realistic. Leaders, in the sense in which it is being used here, are also men and women of integrity. They do not use people; they collaborate with them. They are not mindlessly committed to their agendas. Rather they realize that their agendas will move forward only if others make it happen.

The CEO of ABC is refreshingly direct and honest in communicating his agenda to both internal and external stakeholders. He tells people that his agenda is not meant for the lazy or fainthearted and that he will be as demanding of others as he is of himself. He discusses past successes and failures frankly. He promises employees a robust airline and a share in its profits.

4. CLIMATE OF LEARNING: Leaders create a climate of learning, innovation, and problem solving around their agendas. They create a ferment around their agendas. This ferment moves beyond mere initial enthusiasm. Their agendas bring out the creativity of those involved in developing and implementing them. The agendas stimulate learning in terms of new options and problem solving in terms of moving obstacles out of the way.

The new CEO of ABC walks around selling his strategy. He challenges his managers to come up with ways of driving the strategy

down into the guts of the system while promoting pride of involvement and improved quality of work life. All managers are to provide innovation time every week—that is, work time during which
the only task is to come up with better ways of doing things, especially
servicing customers. Younger managers respond readily and form
quality circles in their units. Older managers are more hesitant, but
the best of them feel a dormant creativity beginning to reassert itself.
More good ideas for increasing productivity are generated over two
months than were previously generated in five years.

5. PERSISTENCE: **Leaders are persistent; they see agendas
through to completion.** Leaders do not let go. They get things done.
They create incentive and reward systems that support both the pursuit and completion of agendas. In one sense, they do not know the
meaning of failure. If they cannot move one way, they will move
another. Setbacks, possibly; but failure, no. Part of leadership involves
making sure that the institutional incentives and rewards for per-
sisting are in place and that they are tailored to individuals.

ABC's CEO is rebuffed in his first attempt to take over a smaller
carrier. The takeover is seen as hostile, and poison-pill strategies are
used by the targeted carrier. He learns from this experience, adopts
a less aggressive approach, engages in quiet partnership talks with
a second carrier, and is successful.

Figure 17-2 illustrates this task-cycle approach to leadership, but
in this case the outcomes are innovative ways of doing things or
system-enhancing business or organizational change.

This kind of "doing" leadership can be found, in different ways,
at *all* levels in companies and institutions. Figure 17-3 presents a
leadership matrix or grid with the different kinds of leaders—
executives, managers, supervisors, professional or technical people,
and operators—along one axis and the five activities listed above on
the other axis. Each cell would indicate how a person exercising
leadership in a specific role might act.

Executive/Executive-Team Leadership

At an executive level, leaders develop broad visions for the company
or institution based on an intimate knowledge of the system itself

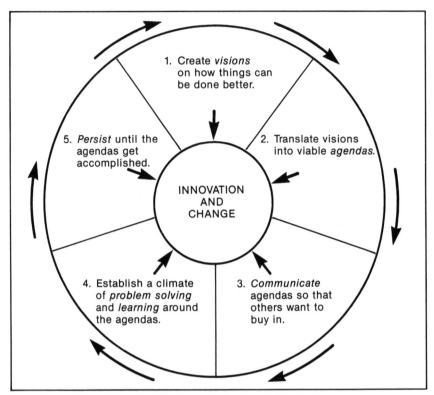

Figure 17-2. The Leadership-Task Cycle

and a practical understanding of environmental happenings, trends, and crises. They are especially innovative in the area of strategy. They also tend to be resource getters—bringing key players on board, identifying new sources for funding, and keeping an eye out for acquisitions. In larger organizations senior managers see themselves as having three roles: managers of their own units, members of the executive team of the divisions in which their units are located, and advisers to the company or institution itself. Some of the ways in which the new CEO of ABC Airways is exercising executive leadership are outlined above.

The following are some questions that can be asked about executive leadership in any company or institution:

- To what degree is our chief executive a person of vision?
- What kind of vision and creativity is found among the chief executive's top team?

TASK CYCLE	LEVELS				
	Executive	Managerial	Supervisory	Professional/ Technical	Operator
1. Vision					
2. Agenda					
3. Commun- ication					
4. Climate of Learning					
5. Persist- ence					

Figure 17-3. Leadership Grid

- How creative are the agendas established by the top person or team?
- How well are these agendas communicated to the rest of the organization?
- How enthusiastically do people in the organization rally around these agendas?
- To what degree does the top team establish a ferment of learning and problem solving around the principal agendas of the company or institution?
- How well does the top team support these agendas through incentives and rewards?
- How rewarding is it to help carry out these agendas?
- To what extent do top team members persist in promoting their agendas? How effective are they in follow through?
- To what degree do the members of the organization see these agendas through to completion?

Managerial Leadership

As we have seen, managers coordinate, facilitate, monitor, and control the work flow. They engage in planning, staffing, organizing, providing feedback, and engaging in appraisals of both people and projects. Managers who are leaders are always looking for better ways of doing all of this. The changing role of the middle manager does not catch them by surprise. For instance, some ABC managers hand over much of their monitoring and control functions to computers and search for innovative ways of adding tangible value to the enterprise. The best realize that the name of the new game is not mastering the bureaucracy and engaging in the politics of self-interest (Nulty, 1987), but finding new ways of managing resources, processes, and people. The director of engineering sets up a task force whose objective is not to explore problems (they know what they are) but to find ways of doing things better. The challenge is lower-cost, higher-quality engineering.

The following are key questions in determining the leadership of a manager:

- In what ways does this manager express managerial vision? establish creative agendas? motivate subordinates? establish a climate of learning and problem solving in the unit? persist in getting things done?

- To what degree does this manager make sure that the mission of the next higher unit and of the company or institution is communicated to the troops?

- How well does this manager see himself or herself as a manager of productivity-related innovation and change?

- What productivity and QWL innovations has this manager instituted?

- How creatively does this manager go about ordinary managerial tasks? planning creatively? organizing creatively? coordinating creatively? facilitating creatively? instituting creative control systems?

- How effectively does this manager establish productivity-related incentives and rewards in the unit?

- How effectively does this manager collaborate with subordinates in setting performance objectives?
- How effectively has this manager established a "culture of feedback" in his or her unit?
- How effectively does this manager use coaching or counseling as a way of adding value to the work done by people in his or her unit?
- How well does this manager protect his or her subordinates from internal and external threats?
- How effective a mentor is this manager?
- How creatively does this manager interact with managers of other units?
- How creatively does this manager do the hard things in his or her unit, such as giving hard messages, letting people go, and cutting costs?
- How creatively does this manager manage the financial and material resources of the unit?
- How creatively does this manager manage his or her subordinate managers?
- How well does this manager manage his or her relationship with the boss?
- What does this manager need to do to become an exemplar manager? to what degree is this possible?

Supervisory Leadership

Leadership, as described by the five activities outlined earlier, can also be found at the supervisory level. For instance, one supervisor in the reservations department of ABC has a vision of reservation-department *teams*, each having a say in the way things are to be done. She institutes something akin to quality circles in order to explore the problems reservationists face and ways of making their work life both more productive and more enjoyable. They produce a list of common problems that arise in conversations with passengers and brainstorm ways of managing them. A common problem is the vast array of fares. They come up with what they need fare-related computer programs to do and pass their requests on to the information services department through their director. Since some supervisors are mini-managers, some of the questions under managerial leadership might be relevant. For others, the following questions might suffice:

- In what ways does this supervisor express vision? establish creative agendas? motivate operators in his or her unit? get operators to learn and solve problems?
- How aware is this supervisor of the mission of this unit? of the company or institution?
- How much of a "sense of people" does this supervisor have?
- How effective are his or her people skills?
- What supervisory innovations has this supervisor introduced?
- What does this supervisor need to do to become an exemplar supervisor? To what degree is this possible?
- In what ways have operators grown under his or her supervision?
- To what degree are supervisors encouraged to innovate?

Professional/Technical Leadership

Professional and technical leaders are on the cutting edge in two ways. First of all, they stay abreast of or even contribute to innovations in their fields. Second (and this is of the essence of professional/technical leadership) they know how to *adapt* innovations to the business and organizational needs of the system. For instance, once the accounting division of ABC has its operations computerized, it offers a range of products to the other units of the airline to help them cut costs and run more efficiently. It shows managers how the cost of hiring consultants in many cases is higher than training internal people to do the same jobs. This enables some departments to cut down on consultants' fees while providing greater job satisfaction for their own members. The following questions are relevant for professional or technical leaders:

- How well does this professional stay abreast of the developments in his or her field?
- In what ways has he or she contributed to the field?
- How effectively does this professional adapt what is new in the field to the needs of this company or institution?
- What kind of model for others is this professional?
- How effectively does this professional teach/train others in the organization?

Operator Leadership

In companies and organizational subunits with a culture of leadership, everyone is encouraged to propose work innovations and organization-enhancing change. A culture of leadership at the operator level can be fostered by participative-management programs. The vice president in charge of refining for one of the large oil companies said that to be a leader in the industry today, they have to squeeze every last ounce of distillate from every barrel of crude. Then he said that some of their best ideas come from hourly workers and that the company needs to learn how to tap into and reward their expertise more effectively. The Paul Revere Insurance Company (Townsend, 1986) encourages everyone to find better ways of doing things and rewards those who do. One of ABC Airways' baggage handlers came up with an idea for a new baggage-flow system that saves both time and work. His idea, modified by some engineers, was incorporated into the baggage-handling system in ABC's facilities in one of its new hubs.

The following questions are relevant for operators in any organization:

- Who are the exemplar operators in this organization and what makes them stand apart?
- To what degree are operators given incentives to find more effective ways of doing their work?
- What kinds of ideas do operators offer?
- What could be done to help operators become more creative?

- How do operators experience the "geometry" of the organization? In what ways do they see themselves on the cutting edge rather than on the bottom?
- What kind of attention and respect do operators in this organization receive?

EPILOGUE

If you are designing a company or some unit, project, or program within it, the framework presented in these pages should help you do so intelligently, even creatively. However, it is up to you to determine which package of the elements discussed here are most relevant to your endeavor. If, on the other hand, you are assessing the effectiveness of your system with a view to improving it, this model should help you both see where the system falls short of the canons of excellence and determine what needs to be done to bring about improvement. Again, you cannot focus on everything. You need to determine which improvement package offers you and the system the most hope. Once you see the need for change, the second volume in this series (*Change-Agent Skills B: Innovation and Change*) provides a complementary framework for understanding, planning, and implementing change.

References

Adventuresome year: United medical grows beyond its original mission. (1986, March 17). *Barron's*, pp. 54-55.

Airfreight carriers: Now you see lots, soon you won't. (1986, December 15). *Business Week*, p. 34.

Albrecht, K., & Zemke, R. (1985). *Service America: Doing business in the new economy*. Homewood, IL: Dow Jones-Irwin.

Aldrich, H. E. (1979). *Organizations and environments*. Englewood Cliffs, NJ: Prentice-Hall.

Archibald, R. (1976). *Managing high technology programs and projects*. New York: John Wiley.

Argyris, C. (1982). *Reasoning, learning, and action: Individual and organizational*. San Francisco: Jossey-Bass.

Beckhard, R. (1985). *Managing change in organizations: Participant's workbook*. Reading, MA: Addison-Wesley.

Bennis, W., & Nanus, B. (1985). *Leaders: The strategies for taking charge*. New York: Harper & Row.

Brethower, D. M. (1972). *Behavioral analysis in business and industry: A total performance system*. Kalamazoo, MI: Behaviordelia.

Brownstein, V. (1987, March 16). Fortune forecast: Don't buy predictions of a growth spurt. *Fortune*, pp.47-48.

Bylinsky, G. (1986, May 26). A breakthrough in automating the assembly line. *Fortune*, pp. 64-66.

Carkhuff, R. R. (1974). *Cry twice*. Amherst, MA: Human Resource Development Press.

Carlzon, J. (1987). *Moments of truth*. Cambridge, MA: Ballinger.

Catalanello, R. F., & Kirkpatrick, D. L. (1968). Evaluating training programs: The state of the art. *Training and Development Journal, 22*, 2-9.

Clifford, D. K. (1981, May). Building a strategic capability. Paper presented at the McGraw-Hill/*Business Week* Strategic Planning and Management Conference, Chicago.

Conn, S. (1986, April 21). Marketing strategy belongs in the business plan. *Crain's Chicago Business*, pp. 27-29.

Creativity for the masses. (1987). *Training: The Magazine of Human Resources Development, 24*(7), 12, 15.

Crosby, P. B. (1980). *Quality is free.* New York: New American Library.

Crosby, P. B. (1984). *Quality without tears.* New York: New American Library.

Davis, S. M. (1987). *Future perfect.* Reading, MA: Addison-Wesley.

Dessler, G. (1976). *Organization and management.* Englewood Cliffs, NJ: Prentice-Hall.

Dunnette, M. D., & Borman, W. C. (1979). Personnel selection and classification systems. In M. R. Rosenweig & L. W. Porter (Eds.), *Annual Review of Psychology, 30*, 477-525.

Dyer, W. G. (1987). *Team building: Issues and alternatives* (2nd ed.). Reading, MA: Addison-Wesley.

Egan, G. (1986). *The skilled helper.* Monterey, CA: Brooks/Cole.

Egan, G. (1988). *Change-agent skills B: Managing innovation and change.* San Diego, CA: University Associates.

Emery, F. E. & Trist, E. L. (1975). *The causal texture of organizational environment. Human Relations, 18*, 21-32.

Even the elite clinics are shopping for patients. (1987, March 24). *Business Week,* pp. 86, 88.

Federal Express delivers a price shock. (1987, March 30). *Business Week,* p. 31.

Feuding among the ruins of failed shock. (1987, May 18). *Business Week,* p. 116.

Finkler, S. A. (1983). *The complete guide to finance and accounting for nonfinancial managers.* Englewood Cliffs, NJ: Prentice-Hall.

Fisher, R., & Ury, W. (1981). *Getting to yes: Negotiating agreement without giving in.* Boston, MA: Houghton Mifflin.

Fix, J. L. (1986, June 16). Twelve o'clock low. *Forbes,* p. 58.

Flatow, P. (1986, September 22). Beyond "me-too"-ism: Being second isn't all bad. *Adweek,* pp. 40, 42.

Fleming, M. M. K. (1984). *Managerial accounting and control techniques for the non-accountant.* New York: Van Nostrand Reinhold.

Fox, W. M. (1987). *Effective group problem sovling.* San Francisco: Jossey-Bass.

Fusco, J., & Posner, B. (1982). *Project planning and management.* Santa Clara, CA: Technical Pathways.

Galante, S. P. (1986, June 30). Distributors bow to demands of "just-in-time" delivery. *The Wall Street Journal,* p. 25.

Galbraith, J. R. (1977). *Organization design.* Reading, MA: Addison-Wesley.

Gilbert, T. F. (1978). *Human competence: Engineering worthy performance.* New York: McGraw-Hill.

Gilbreath, R. D. (1986). *Winning at project management: What works, what fails and why.* New York: John Wiley.

Goldstein, I. L. (1980). Training and organizational psychology. *Professional Psychology, 11,* 421-427.

Goodman, J. (1986, August 18-24). Eyelab sale shows why Quaker nixed specialty retailing. *Crain's Chicago Business,* p. 1.

Groocock, J. M. (1986). *The chain of quality: Market dominance through product superiority.* New York: John Wiley.

Guest, R. H. (1986). Management imperatives for the year 2000. *California Management Review, 28*(4), 62-70.

Guion, R. M. (1976). Recruiting, selection, and job placement. In M. D. Dunnette (Ed.), *Handbook of industrial and organizational psychology.* New York: John Wiley.

Haas, E. A. (1987, March-April). Breakthrough manufacturing. *Harvard Business Review,* pp. 75-81.

Hackman, J. R., & Oldham, G. R. (1980). *Work redesign.* Reading, MA: Addison-Wesley.

Hall, R. H. (1972). *Organizations: Structures and processes.* Englewood Cliffs, NJ: Prentice-Hall, 1972.

Hannafin, M. J., & Witt, J. C. (1983). System intervention and the school psychologist: Maximizing interplay among roles and functions. *Professional Psychology, 14,* 128-136.

Hayes, R. H., & Clark, K. B. (1986, September-October). Why some factories are more productive than others. *Harvard Business Review,* pp. 66-73.

Herzberg, F. (1987, September-October). One more time: How do you motivate employees? *Harvard Business Review,* pp. 109-120. (Original work published 1968.)

Hornung, M. (1987, April 6). United adds lavish service in bid to boost Pacific routes. *Crain's Chicago Business,* p. 4.

Janis, I. L., and Mann, L. (1977). *Decision making: A psychological analysis of conflict, choice, and commitment.* New York: Free Press.

Jereski, L. (1987, April 20). Mystery profits. *Forbes,* p. 54.

Johnson, C. R. (1986, January). An outline for team building. *Training,* pp. 48-52.

Juran, J. M. (1985). *Juran on quality planning.* Wilton, CT: Juran Institute.

Kanter, R. M. (1983). *Change masters: Innovation for productivity in the American corporation.* New York: Simon & Schuster.

Keefe, L. M. (1987, June 29). More room at the top. *Forbes*, pp. 102-103.

Kellog, M. S., & Burstiner, I. (1979). *Putting management theories to work.* Englewood Cliffs, NJ: Prentice-Hall.

Kelly, J. E. (1982). *Scientific management, job redesign, and work performance.* New York: Academic Press.

Kilburg, R. (1978). Consumer survey as needs-assessment method: A case study. *Evaluation and Program Planning, 1,* 284-292.

Kleinfield, N. R. (1982, June 6). A human resource at Allied Corporation. *The New York Times,* p. F4.

Knaus, W. A., Draper, E. A., Wagner, D. P., & Zimmerman, J. E. (1986). An evaluation of outcome from intensive care in major medical centers. *Annals of Internal Medicine, 104,* 410-418.

Kormanski, C., & Mozenter, A. (1987). A new model for team building: A technology for today and tomorrow. In J. W. Pfeiffer (Ed.), *The 1987 annual: Developing human resources.* San Diego, CA: University Associates.

Kotter, J. (1978). *Organizational dynamics: Diagnosis and intervention.* Reading, MA: Addison-Wesley.

Likert, R. (1961). *New patterns of management.* New York: McGraw-Hill.

Likert, R. (1967). *Human organization: Its management and value.* New York: McGraw-Hill.

Lippitt, R. (1979). A human energy issue: The temporary mobilization and use of human resources. *Group and Organization Studies, 4,* 309-315.

Lorey, W. (1983). P.E.R.T.: It's more versatile than you think. *Training: The Magazine of Human Resources Development, 20*(3), 86.

Los Angeles County Public Administrator (1986). Producing more for less. *Administrative Management, 47*(3), 30.

Luthans, F., & Kreitner, R. (1975). *Organizational behavior modification.* Glenview, IL: Scott, Foresman.

Mack, T. (1987, September 21). Orderly mind in a disorderly market. *Forbes*, pp. 62, 64, 66.

Management discovers the human side of automation. (1986, September 29). *Business Week*, pp. 70-76.

Martin, C. C. (1976). *Project management.* New York: AMACOM.

Mason, R. O., & Mitroff, I. I. (1981). *Challenging strategic planning assumptions.* New York: John Wiley.

McLuhan, M. (1964). *Understanding media: The extensions of man.* New York: McGraw-Hill.

Merwin, J. (1986, June 16). A tale of two worlds. *Forbes*, pp. 101-106.

Metcalf, E. I., Riffle, L. V., & Seabury, F., III. (1981, May). Environmental scanning: What is it—Who needs it—How to use it. Workshop presented by *Business Week* on Strategic Planning, Chicago.

Meyer, M. W., et al. (1978). *Environments and organizations.* San Francisco: Jossey-Bass.

Miles, R. H. (1980). *Macro organizational behavior.* Santa Monica, CA: Goodyear.

Miller, G. A., Galanter, E., & Pribam, K. H. (1960). *Plans and the structure of behavior.* New York: Holt, Rinehart, and Winston.

Miller, L. R. (1974). *A peek at PERT.* Escondido, CA: The Center for Leadership Studies.

Miller, L. M. (1978). *Behavior management: The new science of managing people at work.* New York: John Wiley.

Moore, T. (1987, March 16). Why Martin Marietta loves Mary Cunningham. *Fortune.*

Multifoods is ditching its "mishmash of little businesses." (1986, September 22). *Business Week,* p. 34.

Nadler, D. A., & Tushman, M. L. (1977). A diagnostic model for organizational behavior. In J. R. Hackman, E. E. Lawler, & L. W. Porter (Eds.), *Perspectives on behavior in organizations.* New York: McGraw-Hill.

Naisbitt, J. (1982). *Megatrends: Ten new directions transforming our lives.* New York: Warner Books.

Naisbitt, J., & Aburdene, P. (1985). *Re-inventing the corporation.* New York: Warner Books.

Nicholls, H. G. (1981, May). Instituting a strategic management capability. Paper and workshop presented at the McGraw-Hill/*Business Week* Strategic Planning and Management Conference, Chicago.

Nulty, P. (1987, February 2). The economy of the 1990s: How managers will manage. *Fortune,* pp. 47-50.

Odiorne, G. S. (1984). *Srategic management of human resources: A portfolio approach.* San Francisco: Jossey-Bass.

O'Toole, J. (1985). *Vanguard management: Redesigning the corporate future.* New York: Doubleday.

Parkinson, C. N. (1986). *Parkinson's law or the pursuit of progress.* Harmondsworth, England: Penguin. (Original work published 1957.)

Pascale, R. T., & Athos, A. G. (1981). *The art of Japanese management.* New York: Simon & Schuster.

Pearce, J. A., II, & David, F. (1987, May). Corporate mission statements: The bottom line. *Academy of Management Executive, 1,* 109-116.

Pearson, A. E. (1987, July-August). Muscle built the organization. *Harvard Business Review,* pp. 49-55.

People to watch. (1987, March 16). *Fortune*, p. 74.

Peter, L. J., & Hull, R. (1970). *The Peter principle.* New York: Bantam.

Peters, T. (1987). *Thriving on chaos: A revolutionary agenda for today's manager.* New York: Alfred A. Knopf.

Peters, T. J., & Austin, N. (1985). *A passion for excellence: The leadership difference.* New York: Random House.

Peters, T. J., & Waterman, R. W., Jr. (1982). *In search of excellence: Lessons from America's best-run companies.* New York: Harper & Row.

Pfeiffer, J. W., Goodstein, L. D., & Nolan, T. M. (1985). *Understanding applied strategic planning: A manager's guide.* San Diego, CA: University Associates.

Pfeiffer, J. W., Goodstein, L. D., & Nolan, T. M. (1986). *Applied strategic planning: A how to do it guide.* San Diego, CA: University Associates.

Pinchot, G., III. (1985). *Intrapreneuring.* New York: Harper & Row.

Port, O. (1986, March 3). Detecting breakdowns before they occur. *Business Week*, p. 90.

Quaker is feeling its oats again. (1986, September 22). *Business Week*, pp. 80-81.

Reynolds, M. (1982). Learning the ropes. *Society, 19*(6), 30-33.

Ricks, T. E. (1987, April 3). Branching out: Attentive to service, Barnett Banks grows fast, keeps profits up. *The Wall Street Journal*, pp. 1, 23.

Robert, M. (1982). *Managing conflict from the inside out.* San Diego, CA: University Associates.

Robertson, I. T., & Smith, M. (1985). *Motivation and job design: Theory, research, and practice.* London: Institute of Personnel Management.

Robson, M. (1986). *Journey to excellence.* Chichester, England: John Wiley.

Roeber, R. J. C. (1973). *The organization in a changing environment.* Reading, MA: Addison-Wesley.

Rosen, S., & Tesser, A. (1970). On the reluctance to communicate undesirable information: The MUM effect. *Sociometry, 33*, 253-263.

Rosen, S., & Tesser, A. (1971). Fear of negative evaluation and the reluctance to transmit bad news. *Proceedings of the 79th Annual Convention of the American Psychological Association, 6*, 301-302.

Rubin, L. B. (1976). *Worlds of pain: Life in the working class family.* New York: Basic Books.

Rukeyser, L. (1987, March 15). An MBA malaise is duly reported. *The Chicago Tribune.*

Sandberg-Diment, E. (1986, September 28). The executive computer: Making the right connections. *The New York Times*, p. F16.

Schein, E. H. (1978). Human resource planning and development: A total system. In W. W. Burke (Ed.), *The cutting edge: Current theory and practice in organization development.* San Diego, CA: University Associates.

Schein, E. H. (1985). *Organizational culture and leadership: A dynamic view.* San Francisco: Jossey-Bass.

Schmitt, N. (1976). Social and situational determinants of interview decisions: Implications for the employment interview. *Personnel Psychology, 29,* 70-101.

Sculley, J. (1987, September 14). Sculley's lessons from inside Apple. *Fortune,* pp. 108-118. Excerpted from a book by Sculley, J. (with John A. Byrne, 1987), *Odyssey: Pepsi to Apple. . .A journey of adventure, ideas, and the future.* New York: Harper & Row.

Skinner, B. F. (1953). *Science and human behavior.* New York: Macmillan.

Smith, G. N., & Brown, P. B. (1986). *Sweat equity: What it really takes to build America's best small companies—by the guys who did it.* New York: Simon & Schuster.

Spiro, H. T. (1977). *Finance for the nonfinancial manager.* New York: John Wiley.

Steiner, G. A. (1979). *Strategic planning: What every manager must know.* New York: Free Press.

Sugar and spice and. . . . (1987, June 4). *Financial Weekly* (U.K.), pp. 34-35.

Telling, E. R. (1985). Restructuring for growth. In J. M. Rosow (Ed.), *Views from the top.* New York: Facts on File.

Terkel, S. *Working.* (1974). New York: Pantheon.

Tesser, A., & Rosen, S. (1972). Similarity of objective fate as a determinant of the reluctance to transmit unpleasant information: The MUM effect. *Journal of Personality and Social Psychology, 23,* 46-53.

Tesser, A., Rosen, S., & Batchelor, T. (1972). On the reluctance to communicate bad news (the MUM effect): A role play extension. *Journal of Personality, 40,* 88-103.

Tesser, A., Rosen, S., & Tesser, M. (1971). On the reluctance to communicate undesirable messages (the MUM effect): A field study. *Psychological Reports, 29,* 651-654.

Thomas, K. W. (1976). Conflict and conflict management. In M. D. Dunnette (Ed.), *Handbook of industrial and organizational psychology.* Chicago: Rand McNally.

Thomas, K. W., & Schmidt, W. H. (1976). A survey of managerial interests with respect to conflict. *Academy of Management Journal, 19,* 315-318.

Townsend, P. L. (1986). *Commit to quality.* New York: John Wiley.

Trachtenberg, J. A. (1986, July 14). Shake, rattle, and conk: If this is a service economy, where's the repair service? *Forbes.*

Tsongas, P. (1981). *The road from here: Liberalism and realities in the 1980s.* New York: Alfred A. Knopf.

Walton, R. E. (1987). *Managing conflict: Interpersonal dialogue and third-party roles* (2nd ed.). Reading, MA: Addison-Wesley.

Vaill, P. B. (1980). Commentary on Lundberg's "Teaching organizational development: Some core instructional issues." *Exchange: The Organizational Behavior Teaching Journal, 5*(2), 25-30.

Wanous, J. P. (1980). *Organizational entry.* Reading, MA: Addison-Wesley.

Weisbord, M. R. (1976). Organizational diagnosis: Six places to look for trouble with or without a theory. *Group and Organizational Studies, 1,* 430-447.

Wilson, C. L. (1983). *A guide to good management practices and peer relations.* New Canaan, CT: Clark Wilson.

Wilson, C. L. (1988a). Improving management practices through feedback and training. In J. Jones, B. Steffy, & D. Bray (Eds.), *Applying psychology in business: The manager's handbook.* Lexington, MA: Lexington Books.

Wilson, C. L. (1988b). Task cycle theory: A learning-based view of organization behavior. In R. Ochsman & P. Whitney (Eds.), *Psychology and productivity.* New York: Plenum.

The world's 50 biggest industrial CEOs. (1987, August 3). *Fortune,* pp. 17-60.

Yates, R. E. (1987, February 15). United's Japan hop a perplexing route. *The Chicago Tribune.*

Zawacki, J. (1963). *A system of unofficial rules of a bureaucracy: A study of hospitals.* Unpublished doctoral dissertation, University of Pittsburg.

Zemke, R. (1984). Project management by computer. *Training: The Magazine of Human Resources Development, 21*(3), 48-53.

Zemke, R. (1986a). Contact! Training employees to meet the public. *Training: The Magazine of Human Resources Development, 23*(8), 41-45.

Zemke, R. (1986b). The Pareto principle: Why things aren't fair. *Training: The Magazine of Human Resources Development, 23*(7), 59-60.

Name Index

Subject Index

Action plans, 34-36, 96
Appraisal, 106, 130, 162-163
Assumption of authority, 120
Audiovisual equipment,
    as a material resource, 94
Avoidance behavior, 179-180

Behavior modification, 171
Business dimensions of model A,
    4-5
Business environment, 4, 27-37
    charting, 33
    general, 4, 28-30, 58
    interpenetration of system
      and, 32
    managing, 33-36
    scanning, 33-34
    specific, 30-32
    and systems resources, 35
Business plan, 61, 101
Business values and policies, 43-46
Business vs. organization, 2-3
    managers of processes in,
      191-192

CETA work program, 80
Chain of quality, 70
Clients and customers, 17-25
    needs and wants of, 21-25
    service, 71-74
Committed pluralists, 89

Communications, 111, 157-170
    appraisal, 162-163
    conflict management, 157, 160,
      167-170
    by effective leadership, 197
    feedback, 89, 106, 127, 128, 134,
      138, 157, 160-163, 172, 173,
      176, 192, 193
    information sharing, 157, 176
    interpersonal, 157, 169, 170
    interunit, 157, 169, 170
    in Model A, 6
    MUM effect, 161
    problem solving, 142, 149, 157,
      163-166, 168
    technology, 159
Competence 125-144, 158
    in Model A, 6, 111
Competent units, 125-130
    examples of, 125-129
    determining competency level of,
      129-130
Computers, 159-160
    as material resource, 94-95
Conflict management, 157, 167-169
    negotiation, 167-168
    outcomes 167, 169
Consumerism, 68
"Culture cards," 41
Customer-friendly systems, 72-73
Customers. See Clients and
    customers

217